SECOND EDITION

OWNING UP

To every adult who sees the heart, wisdom, and potential in every child

SECOND EDITION

OWNING UP

EMPOWERING ADOLESCENTS TO CONFRONT SOCIAL CRUELTY, BULLYING, AND INJUSTICE

ROSALIND WISEMAN

Foreword by Richard Weissbourd

A JOINT
PUBLICATION

CORWIN
A SAGE Publishing Company

AMLE

FOR INFORMATION:

Corwin
A SAGE Company
2455 Teller Road
Thousand Oaks, California 91320
(800) 233-9936
www.corwin.com

SAGE Publications Ltd.
1 Oliver's Yard
55 City Road
London EC1Y 1SP
United Kingdom

SAGE Publications India Pvt. Ltd.
B 1/I 1 Mohan Cooperative Industrial Area
Mathura Road, New Delhi 110 044
India

SAGE Publications Asia-Pacific Pte. Ltd.
3 Church Street
#10-04 Samsung Hub
Singapore 049483

Program Director: Jessica Allan
Senior Associate Editor: Kimberly Greenberg
Editorial Assistant: Katie Crilley
Production Editor: Melanie Birdsall
Copy Editor: Talia Greenberg
Typesetter: C&M Digitals (P) Ltd.
Proofreader: Ellen Howard
Cover Designer: Gail Buschman
Marketing Manager: Jill Margulies

Printed in the United States of America

Library of Congress Cataloging-in-Publication Data

Names: Wiseman, Rosalind, author.

Title: Owning up : empowering adolescents to confront social cruelty, bullying, and injustice / Rosalind Wiseman ; foreword by Richard Weissbourd.

Other titles: Owning up curriculum

Description: Second edition. | Thousand Oaks, California : Corwin, [2017] | Includes bibliographical references.

Identifiers: LCCN 2016021966 | ISBN 9781506343679 (pbk. : alk. paper)

Subjects: LCSH: Teenagers—United States—Life skills guides. | Teenagers—United States—Attitudes. | Teenagers—United States—Conduct of life. | Adolescent psychology.

Classification: LCC HQ796 .W535 2017 | DDC 305.235—dc23 LC record available at https://lccn.loc.gov/2016021966

This book is printed on acid-free paper.

Certified Chain of Custody
Promoting Sustainable Forestry
www.sfiprogram.org
SFI-01268
SUSTAINABLE FORESTRY INITIATIVE
SFI label applies to text stock

16 17 18 19 20 10 9 8 7 6 5 4 3 2 1

Contents

Appendices

 Visit the companion website at
www.owningup.online

Foreword

Throughout history, Americans have tended to look to schools to develop ethical character in students. These days, the need for schools to shoulder at least part of that responsibility seems especially urgent. Rates of bullying, sexual harassment, and cruelty in schools are high, and our public life is rife with incivility and contempt—a state of things that speaks loudly to our failure to instill in children both respect for those who are different from them in ideology and background and a commitment to the common good.

Yet the unhappy reality is that far too often, schools fail in this task. It's not for want of trying: Schools across the country have undertaken legions of programs designed to address cruelty and promote caring and respect, including antibullying, character education, conflict resolution, youth development, and social-emotional learning programs. But with some important exceptions, there's little evidence that these programs reach students in meaningful ways or develop in them any greater, lasting sense of responsibility for others or their communities. Too often, in fact, students experience these programs as dreary and condescending and become adept at simply parroting back what adults want to hear.

That's why I was delighted to read Rosalind Wiseman's curriculum, *Owning Up.*

Wiseman is one of the great American chroniclers of young people's lives. She has spent decades talking to teenagers, never shying away from the most tender and difficult topics, whether bullying, cliques, or sexual harassment. She has shown us how ornate teens' social lives can be, and how little adults often know about these intricacies. She has logged many hours in schools and understands the complex, wonderful, daunting work of teaching. Her curriculum is mindful both of what can go wrong in difficult classroom conversations— she is alert to the landmines—and of what can go wonderfully, beautifully right.

What makes me most hopeful about *Owning Up* is that unlike many attempts to instill character in young people, Wiseman doesn't want teachers to lecture or hector. She wants them, first and foremost, to listen and understand how teenagers make sense of their world. She knows that you can't pry open a teenager's head and pour in virtues. Teenagers, like the rest of us, want to be valued for what they value in themselves—their capacity to think. They are far more likely to "own up," to better understand and manage their feelings and to take responsibility for their actions, if adults take the risk of respecting their thinking and engaging them in probing—and, to use Wiseman's word, "messy"—conversation. Teens are also dealing, sometimes daily, with enormously complex moral dilemmas, situations where values and loyalties come in conflict. They may be struggling, for example, with whether to be *loyal* to a friend who was cruel to another student on Facebook or *honest* with a teacher who asks them who the perpetrator is. These conflicts won't be solved by the usual platitudes, by simply telling students to respect others. Students' capacity to act with decency and care depends on their ability to use their intelligence, parsing and appreciating multiple perspectives and values.

Crucially, Wiseman recognizes as well that for teens to "own up," adults need to "own up" as well. Too many character education and antibullying efforts miss the central fact that children's social, emotional, and ethical growth is less a matter of the lessons in a curriculum or a text than of students' day-to-day relationships with each other and with their teachers. How students develop capacity for care, empathy, and fairness is deeply interwoven with adults' capacity for empathy and fairness. For better or worse, teachers influence students' emotional and ethical growth by how fairly they balance different students' needs, how they define students' obligations to each other, and how they treat students who irritate or anger them. Teachers can make children radioactive with shame or demonstrate the kind of empathy that generates deep concern for others and those different from them.

Wiseman's curriculum is thus a journey for both students and teachers. She wants teachers to wade into themselves and to ask hard questions about how their own identities and histories, including their past experiences with teasing, bullying, discrimination, and power, shape their interactions with students. She knows that self-observing and self-monitoring teachers—teachers who are able, in her phrase, to "check their baggage"—are more able to truly know their students and respond to them with real and deep empathy, uncluttered by their own past angers and wounds. She wants, too, for teachers to do something that adults who interact with children often never do: think hard about how students perceive them. She asks teachers to consider this type of question: "What characteristics do you have that would discourage any student from approaching you when they need help?"

None of this would matter, though, if Wiseman didn't create a curriculum that engages students. *Owning Up* takes up topics that other curriculums tend not to touch and that meet students where they live and breathe. Students discuss, for instance, crushes, physical appearance, gossip, and the importance of "reputation." Rather than creating a curriculum composed of what adults think young people *ought* to talk about, Wiseman has created a curriculum based on the rich learning that can take place when teachers start with what students are *actually* occupied with. Students are able to step back and examine the emotionally layered and ethically charged drama of their own lives.

Wiseman has not set out an easy task for either teachers or students, but that is a mark of her courage and honesty. There are no easy roads to leading a humane and decent life, and students should experience that true care, decency, and responsibility for others often come from struggle. We should be very thankful to Wiseman that she has faced that fact squarely. And we should be thankful to her for providing such a clear and accessible map to teachers for navigating that struggle. The world will be a better place if this map finds a home in schools across the country.

—**Richard Weissbourd**
Senior Lecturer and Director of the
Human Development and Psychology Program
Co-Director, Making Caring Common Project
Harvard Graduate School of Education

Acknowledgments

Every book and curriculum I write for and about young people depends on field experts looking over everything I do and then giving me a lot of suggestions about what to change. This project was no exception. So huge thank-yous to the *Owning Up* editors: Dru Tomlin, Charlie Kuhn, Tessa Peterson, Jesse Van Divier, Lizzy Dietrick, Carey Goldstein, Shanterra McBride, Timmy Dolan, Marcos Ospina, Grace Milijasevic, Jesse Shafroth, Anne Clifford, Susan Metzler, Winston Robinson, Dre Gambrell, and Ricki Coston. Thank goodness you all were on board—I am so grateful for your time, advice, and ongoing commitment.

About the Author

 **Rosalind Wiseman** has had only one job since she graduated from college—to help communities shift the way we think about children and teens' emotional and physical well-being. As a teacher, thought leader, author, and media spokesperson on bullying, ethical leadership, the use of social media, and media literacy, she is in constant dialogue and collaboration with educators, parents, children, and teens.

Most famously, Rosalind is the author of *Queen Bees and Wannabes: Helping Your Daughter Survive Cliques, Gossip, Boyfriends, and the New Realities of Girl World*—the groundbreaking, best-selling book that was the basis for the movie *Mean Girls*. The fully revised third edition was published in July 2016.

Rosalind's other publications include *Masterminds and Wingmen: Helping Our Boys Cope With Schoolyard Power, Locker-Room Tests, Girlfriends, and the New Rules of Boy World*, which was awarded Best Parenting Book by Books for a Better Life in 2014. She is also a regular curriculum contributor to the Anti-Defamation League.

From teaching in the classroom to large keynote presentations, each year Rosalind works with tens of thousands of students, educators, parents, counselors, coaches, and administrators to create communities based on the belief that each person has a responsibility to treat themselves and others with dignity. Rosalind has presented at the White House, the American School Counselor Association, South by Southwest, the Game Developers Conference, the International Boys' Schools Coalition, the American Association of School Administrators, and countless schools throughout the United States and abroad. She is an advisor to the U.S. Department of Health and Human Services' Substance Abuse and Mental Health Services Administration.

A native of Washington, D.C., she currently lives in Colorado with her husband and two sons.

Introduction

The Partners

The Association for Middle Level Education (AMLE) is committed to helping middle grade educators reach every student, grow professionally, and create great schools. It helps all students ages 10 to 15 succeed as learners and make positive contributions to their communities and to the world.

Corwin has one objective and one objective only: to help educators do their important work better.

Creating Cultures of Dignity is an organization founded by educator Rosalind Wiseman that works with communities to shift the way we think about children and teens' emotional and physical well-being.

Together, we work to help people—students, teachers, families, and community members—to understand the academic, social, and emotional complexities of young adolescence and middle level education. We envision a school in which educators are self-reflective, passionate, and capable of walking alongside our students as they navigate their adolescence and education so they, too, can reach their social, emotional, and academic potential.

Welcome to the Program!

Owning Up is a tool to help you work with the most interesting, funny, and challenging people in the world: tweens and teens. It's also a tool to teach young people the capacity to understand their individual development in relation to group behavior with their peers, the social dynamics that lead to discrimination and bigotry, and the skills to be socially competent in the difficult yet common social conflicts they experience.

Whether you're teaching *Owning Up* in a school, a team, or a youth-serving organization, what you have in your hands is a flexible, dynamic curriculum that respects your knowledge of the young people you work with and the communities you operate in.

That said, *Owning Up* does have core principles, and we assume that educators who will implement *Owning Up* agree with the following:

- We are in partnership with the young people we work with, and they are often our best teachers.
- A young person's academic success and engagement is interconnected with their social competency.

- "Soft skills"—the ability to work with others, negotiate conflict, and understand and respect the needs of others in balance with one's own needs—is a difficult skill set to master and requires constant and graduated practice.

- To be credible and effective educators, adults must self-reflect on how they interact with young people. A culture of dignity is impossible if the adults don't hold themselves to the same standards they demand of their students.

- No community is immune from abuses of power. But just as true is the possibility that any community can effectively address even the worst injustices that can occur within it.

Owning Up examines the cultural constructs that influence young people's socialization. It incorporates cultural definitions of gender, sexism, racism, classism, homophobia, and other forms of "isms" that affect young people's beliefs and decision making around self-esteem, friendships, group dynamics, and social and physical aggression.

But if you've taught this age group before, you know that implementing *Owning Up,* or any program like it, can be challenging because young people are rightfully skeptical. They have endured unrealistic assemblies or character-building programs and heard too many superficial slogans that don't reflect the complexity of the issues they face or include them as an essential part of the process to create solutions. Worse, they've interacted with adults who demand their obedience and respect yet don't treat them with the dignity that any person deserves, regardless of age.

In spite of the risk we are asking young people to take, we have seen time and time again that if adults listen to young people before we give them advice, they will take the leap of faith with us. That is also what *Owning Up* is about: collaboration between educators and students to create honest discussion about the issues most challenging to young people to then help them find the courage, passion, and ability to create the world in which they want to live.

Who Teaches *Owning Up*?

We are aware that some educators come to *Owning Up* on their own, while others are told to implement it by a supervisor—sometimes with less guidance and support than they need. We also appreciate how frustrating it can be to be told to lead a program without the necessary resources or time to do your best. What we want you to hear from us is that you know the young people you work with and we've done our best to give you a comprehensive teaching strategy that will empower you and your students. We encourage you to make this curriculum your own. And if you modify an exercise or come up with another way to approach a topic we cover, we want to know about the great innovative ideas you've come up with. Therefore, later in this introduction we will outline the educator support network we have created to make that possible.

About the Sessions

Here's a more specific breakdown of what *Owning Up* covers:

- Identify and discuss behaviors and attitudes associated with groups, popularity, trust, exclusion, and bullying.
- Understand the impact of how one expresses anger and learn strategies to effectively communicate when anxious or in conflict.
- Develop a plan of action when a friend or group demeans one or someone else.
- Recognize the influence of culture on individuals' behavior and decision making, from friendships to academic engagement.
- Develop an understanding of how culture defines gender and race and how that can affect self-concept, self-expression, and interactions with others.
- Identify and strengthen support networks and personal standards in relationships.
- Clarify and promote the definition of *consent*—across the spectrum of young people's interactions and relationships.

The *Owning Up* Teaching Strategies

The SEAL Strategy

A primary goal of *Owning Up* is to help students process their "messy" feelings (anger, sadness, frustration, anxiety) into a meaningful, substantive dialogue with another person. In *Owning Up,* this is taught through the SEAL strategy. But like any strategy where young people are asked to put feelings into words and to use those words, the approach is often perceived as unrealistic and "adult speak." So you shouldn't be surprised if you get a lot of resistance from your students when you teach SEAL. They may think you are trying to put words in their mouths, or make them talk like a "robot." When that happens, we have found it helpful to say: "Everyone's probably going to experience a conflict where they lose their words or think of the thing they really wanted to say five minutes after the conversation (or argument) ended. SEAL is just a strategy to figure out how to speak your truth in those situations."

Another way to think about introducing SEAL is to compare it to the students' favorite games. Whether it's a role-playing game, a sports game, an adventure game, or even a first-person shooter game, there are always battles or competitions to be found. To get ready for that moment, a player considers his or her strengths, resources, lay of the land, position, or types of items they could gather—and then considers the same of their opponents: What are their strengths? How will they use the landscape? What are their powers? How can they avoid the lethal blow? The point of the game is to do your best and "level up" so you're more prepared and able to handle different situations the next time you play.

It's the same thing with SEAL. SEAL enables someone to think through their strategy so they have the maximum possibility of handling themselves with mastery in the moment of conflict and discomfort. The "pushback" is the opposing force's response: the things the other person can do to retaliate, put you on the defensive, or create confusion and distraction. The only difference between a battle in a game and using SEAL in real life (and it's a big one) is that instead of the goal being to win (i.e., total destruction of the other team), it's to manage yourself in a conflict where you are taken seriously and you uphold the dignity of all involved. Doing any part of SEAL is a success—even if it's not immediately used to confront the person.

Steps in the SEAL strategy are as follows:

Stop: Breathe, observe, and ask yourself what the situation is about. Decide when and where you can talk to the person so the person will be most likely to listen to you.

Explain: Take your negative feelings and put them into words—be specific about what you don't like and what you want to happen instead. You realize you are making a request, so you know you may not get what you want. But at least you are being clear with yourself and others.

Affirm and acknowledge: State your right to be treated with dignity by the other person and your responsibility to do the same. If appropriate, acknowledge your part in contributing to the situation.

Lock:

- *Lock in the friendship:* Decide to resolve the situation and continue being friends.
- *Take a break:* Decide to take a break from the friendship but agree to talk later about reestablishing the friendship.
- *Lock out the friendship:* Decide that you can't be friends right now.

Even though *Owning Up* is filled with concrete strategies about what to say and do in various situations, these strategies will work only if the students use SEAL to come up with their own words. If they try to precisely follow the script or think that's what we are asking them to do, it won't work. And it's the same for you as the educator. In order to make your teaching efforts authentic and credible to your students, you also have to make *Owning Up* your own.

Labels

In *Owning Up,* you will go through a general breakdown of the different roles people can take in groups. However, placing labels on people's behavior is tricky and can even be counterproductive. No one likes other people to label them. The roles in *Owning Up* are used as a way to identify why a person acts a specific way when they're in a group, and to understand the possible consequences. Ideally, a label is something a person decides to pick and associate with themselves—even if there are negative things connected to that label—because it gives them insight into their behavior and decision making. Likewise, a label should be something a person can take off when it no longer feels right to them because that awareness leads to greater self-knowledge and self-management.

How to Talk About Gender

We discuss gender a lot in *Owning Up,* and that can be complicated as well. Many young people are challenging core assumptions about gender and demanding expanded gender definitions and expressions. At the same time, negative and confining gender stereotypes still permeate our culture and people's interactions with and perceptions of each other. *Owning Up* is taught in diverse communities that have different comfort levels with how a person expresses their gender. Our bottom line is that every person's dignity must be respected. Every student has a right to feel comfortable, safe, and acknowledged.

Specifically, if you teach the session on dating and relationships, we encourage you to state at the beginning that you will be pronoun neutral so that all students feel included without having to "out" themselves. Something you can say is, "I will be doing my best to not be gender specific when we talk about dating or relationships so that all students feel comfortable. And please feel free to make other suggestions so we can do our best to make everyone feel included in the conversation."

Conducting Role Plays

Role-playing can be an excellent teaching tool to get students out of their seats and experiencing the curriculum in a more socially and physically dynamic way. Some educators love it and some don't. Some students love it and some don't. If you're in the camp of not being a huge fan of role plays, that's okay; there's plenty else to do in the sessions. However, you may wish to consider doing them just to get out of your own comfort zone of teaching.

The curriculum offers role plays that reflect students' experiences, but it's critical to ask your students to use scenarios from their own experiences so that they feel comfortable sharing. That being said, sometimes role plays can be too awkward or uncomfortable to play out. If this is the case with your students, you or a student volunteer can read the role-play scenario aloud and use it to generate discussion. Carey Goldstein, a middle school counselor who uses *Owning Up*, encourages you to think about roles plays this way:

> If the kids do not come up with [role plays] on their own I use scenarios that
> are a year or two old so kids do not know which case I am talking about, but I
> can say without a doubt that it happened in our school. This helps when they
> pretend things do not happen here. I stress with the students to be realistic
> and not just act out what they think teachers want to hear.

As the educator, it is your responsibility to choose which students play which roles. When you do this, keep in mind what you know about the individual students. For example, it can be a critical learning opportunity for students who have high social status to play roles in which they don't—and vice versa. In this type of reversal, it is important for you as the educator to make sure they are performing consistently with the role assigned to them, not the role they tend to play in real life. But, in general, the key to an effective role play is to set up the situation and then allow the students to act freely according to what they think is the most realistic portrayal of events.

It is also your responsibility to stop the role play when necessary. The time to stop is when the dynamics you want to get across in the session are revealed. If for any reason you believe the role play is being manipulated by some of the actors to reinforce the social positions in the group, you can stop the role play and conduct the "getting stuck" exercise, described later in this introduction.

Unless otherwise specified, the role plays are intended to be conducted twice: The first time, the students act out the most likely way a situation would occur. The second time, the students act out what should happen to give the subjects power over the situation and ensure that they can speak their truth. Often, this second role play involves SEAL. As part of the process, you can ask them which feels more real and how to work toward getting to the version with SEAL. If the group is really resistant, you can go through each step and ask them to tell you why they think it won't work. Through that process, they realize why it will work, and they buy in.

Bystanders

A *bystander* is defined as "someone who is present at an event but who does not take part." *Owning Up* defines the dynamic of bystanding as more complex. All bystanders have an emotional reaction in the moment, and their reaction is often based on the relationship they have with the target or the aggressor and their place in the social group. In large part in school, the sense of the bystander's obligation to stick up for the target or join the aggressor depends on various dynamics, including how much they like the target or aggressor, the public nature of the situation, and how much they perceive they will suffer if the aggressor turns their attention on them.

Bystanders are frequently convinced to join the person abusing power because they believe they'll sacrifice their position in the group if they speak out. If bystanders are silent (which some define as being neutral), their "nonaction" either looks like support for the person abusing power or sends the message that they're powerless to stop him or her. This isn't to say that being a bystander who speaks out is easy. Far from it. Speaking out against these power dynamics can be terrifying, and young people know this like they know how to breathe.

The bystander issue often arises when students are role-playing—specifically, when you ask students what responsibility they have to stop people from bullying others. If you tell them to imagine, in the scenario, that they are good friends with the target, there is usually a strong motivation to intervene. But if you tell them they don't like or know the target, there is usually no motivation to intervene. Your goal as educator is to reframe the dynamic for the students so that the relationship to the target or the aggressor is not the determining factor in whether students choose to speak up. Sessions 2, 4, 5, and 7 will provide you with more structure regarding how to walk the students through the process, but in general you want to encourage your students to ask themselves the following:

- Do you think you should intervene in some way?
- What is your relationship to the target?
- If your relationship to the target was different than what you have described, would your motivation to intervene change?
- Why does your connection to that person determine if you should intervene?
- Regardless of your answers above, what is an effective strategy to intervene so that the target's dignity is affirmed and they feel some power in the situation?

An ideal bystander recognizes the moment when some kind of intervention is necessary to affirm the dignity and/or physical safety of the target(s), and then acts. That action has countless possibilities, but the lesson to be imparted is to pay attention to the dynamic that is stripping the target of their dignity, to acknowledge the bystander's feelings about what's happening, to affirm the target's dignity, and to reinforce their safety.

Educator Responsibilities

If you love working with young people, if you're okay with throwing out your carefully prepared lesson plan because your students have gotten really engaged in a discussion, and if you don't take it personally when they argue with you, you'll be a great *Owning Up* educator. Too often adults don't want to allow young people to have these uncomfortable conversations, but we think creating an environment where young people can passionately disagree while treating each other with dignity is one of the most important skills they can develop—and one we all benefit from when these young people become adults who can engage in constructive dialogue.

As a general rule, you want to create a learning environment where students can feel uncomfortable but not unsafe. In order to do this, you must first ask yourself how these issues push your own buttons. For example, what experiences of power over others have you had—especially as a young person—that impact your professional and personal life now? Other questions are equally important. If your race is different from that of your students, do you feel comfortable talking to them about racism and different people's experience with race? If you are close to them in age, how does that affect your teaching? Do some of the students intimidate you? Why? How do you handle this dynamic?

To help you with your own self-evaluation, we have included an individual assessment at the end of this Introduction and some "Check Your Baggage" opportunities embedded in the sessions where we ask you questions to help you prepare for the session you are about to teach.

Observe your students both inside and outside the teaching environment. Watch how they walk into the room and take their seats; observe where students group themselves in public spaces (the lunchroom, the hallways, a wall where students hang out); look at where socially powerful students place themselves in relation to adult authority figures. Do socially powerful students stay as far away as possible from a supervising teacher while waiting for the bus after school? Or, in contrast, do they feel comfortable occupying the same space as adults? Observing behavior patterns can give you important insights into the social structures of your students and how they may bring them into your classroom.

Also remember that students participate in different ways. One student will be better at verbal discussions, while another will contribute more comfortably through writing. Each means of expression is equally valid. Just remember to look for opportunities where students will have various ways to share personal experiences.

Creating Connection

It's the small moments of relating to each other that build trust among instructors and students. Effective educators connect, even briefly, with students so each one knows they are seen and acknowledged as a valued member of the community. "Nice shoes!" or "I saw your drawing in art class—it's great!" or a warm hello can make a profound difference.

Listen

Listening means being prepared to be changed by what you hear. At the moments you feel as though you need to talk most, listen. Sometimes you'll want to get through the agenda, but your students will be stuck on a particular topic. What do you do? Although you shouldn't let a personal student experience hijack the session, if your group is engaged and participating, forget your agenda and focus on what they are discussing as the way to achieve the curriculum's overall goals.

A student might ask a question to which you don't know the answer or on which you feel you need to reflect more before answering. If so, tell the class that the question or comment was a good one and that you want time to make sure you are giving the best possible answer. Then begin the next session with, "Last week a student asked a great question that I told you I needed to think about. So before we go on I want to tell you my answer and then you can tell me what you think."

Respect the Power of Their Culture

Familiarize yourself with the books and social media platforms they mention; listen to their music, play their video games even it's just for a few minutes, watch their movies, and notice their style. You don't have to like any of these things, but you do have to acknowledge that there is something in them that your students find compelling. If you don't understand a word they use, ask them to define it. Yes, they'll laugh at you, but you are demonstrating that you care enough about their culture to ask.

Establish Your Ethical Authority

When you value your students' feelings and perspectives, they will feel safe to discuss and disagree about difficult issues and topics. For example, tell your students about good work they've done or positive risks they've taken. Tell them when you disagree. Avoid making comments about their physicality like their height, hair, size, or body type—basically, anything that would make you feel uncomfortable if someone said it to you. If you make a mistake (and we all have), apologizing to them demonstrates what ethical leaders do when they've made a mistake.

Value of Silence

Your students may be quiet when difficult issues are raised or when they think about the issues being presented. Don't be intimidated by silence. Ask your students about it: "Why did it get quiet when we talked about this issue?" Allow your students quiet time to think and reflect, through writing or informal dialogue, as they work through issues that have been raised. In addition, some students may feel more comfortable talking collaboratively in a small group instead of in front of the whole group.

Understand Students' History

Unfortunately, young people often experience adults belittling or underestimating their problems, stressors, and conflicts. Never underestimate the possibility that your students are currently struggling with serious problems. Their experiences shape the attitudes and beliefs they bring to class. On the other side of the coin, your students undoubtedly have untapped potential, positive interests, and hidden talents that may go unrecognized or uncelebrated during the course of the school day, and it is your responsibility to know and honor those triumphs—as you also attend to their challenges.

Seriously . . . Be Uncomfortable

Successful use of the *Owning Up Curriculum* necessitates moments of genuine discomfort for both educators and students. These uncomfortable moments are often essential for genuine learning to take place, but how these moments occur is critical. You must always elicit students' answers. If students are too embarrassed to say aloud what they are thinking, then encourage them to write their thoughts down and give them to you in private. Always remember that especially for younger students, "bad words" can be frightening. If you need to put those words up on the board or flip chart, but it makes your students uncomfortable, explain that you are talking about these words precisely because they are so hurtful. Let students know that you can erase the words after you put them there.

People can also be incredibly uncomfortable talking about "diversity" issues. People give lip service to respecting "difference" all the time. They say platitudes like "everyone is equal," but it's common for adults to be so uncomfortable with these topics that they don't allow young people to wrestle with their thoughts and feelings about these issues—and that stifles any meaningful conversation. There is nothing offensive or wrong about respectfully asking someone to explain something about themselves that you don't understand. If your students say something racist or bigoted, lean into those conversations. *Owning Up* should be a place where it's safe to make "mistakes." If someone says something offensive, that doesn't mean other people have the right to jump on that person and assume the worst. To put it another way, "Be hard on ideas but easy on people."

Let Your Students Get to Know You

It is equally important to let students get to know you. Here are some suggestions.

Manage Impressions

As soon as you walk into the room, your students will know whether you genuinely love working with people their age. They will also know if you are intimidated, want to be a friend and not an adult, or are burnt out. Your students also will know who is in control—you or the most socially powerful students in the group. Groups benefit from parameters, and the procedures presented in Session 1, "Getting Started," are designed to help you establish your authority while making all students feel like they have an important voice in the discussion.

Move Around

Don't get stuck in front of the group, looking as though you are glued to the front of the class. Move around so the students know you are comfortable in their space and excited to be there with them. When a student is being distracting, move nearby so your presence is felt but not in an overbearing way. And remember, you can always experiment with the learning environment. Experiment with different desk configurations that help collaboration and cooperative dialogue: quads, triads, semicircles, and whole circles. A whole circle configuration lessens the power binary between teacher and student because everyone is sitting together without front and back rows, and no teacher is standing at the front.

Share

On occasion, share your own experiences with your students. Don't do it constantly, because then it will come across as if you're "teaching" this program to process your own issues. But if you share strategically, your students will connect with stories about your experiences when you were their age, especially those about when you made mistakes but learned from them. Although you should avoid sharing stories about your life now to maintain boundaries between you and your students, sharing your earlier life experiences makes your relationship with your students more reciprocal and less of an invasion of their privacy. To connect with your students, remember your feelings and thoughts about yourself and your peers at their age. As students share their experiences, you will also remember how you felt when you faced these issues.

Common Challenges

The following describe challenges that commonly arise when teaching *Owning Up*.

Personal Stories

When a student wants to tell a personal story, ask them to leave out the names of the other students involved. Also ask them to avoid very detailed physical descriptions of other students. Not only can this objectify some students, but this is a tactic that some students use when asked not to use names. While it's true that the students may know who is being talked about, it's important to emphasize the focus on the reason why the student believes the story is connected to the session.

It's also common for at least one student to constantly share their personal stories with the rest of the class. While we want to encourage personal reflection, when a student monopolizes the class with personal stories, overall learning suffers. When that happens, focus the student on how the experience they're sharing reflects the overall content and then redirect the class.

Name-Calling

In or outside of the class, you may hear students use degrading comments against one another. When it happens in the session, these words are usually said so quickly that educators may be confused about whether to stop and address the name-calling or continue with the session. We suggest that you quickly stop and ask the following question: "You just said Jason is gay. What does the word *gay* mean to you?" Your students (especially the younger ones) will almost always say, "Stupid. Dumb." Your response is, "By using the word *gay* to put someone down, you are going against the guidelines we all we agreed on. So you may not use that word." That way, you avoid being derailed by a long conversation, you're showing your values in action, and you stop the discriminatory behavior—based on the group's own rules. There are many opportunities throughout the program to further explore the damage these types of words can cause.

Watered-Down Words

Owning Up challenges students to closely examine the definition and meaning of words. It asks educators to challenge themselves in the same way—especially concerning words that they commonly use with young people. For example, *self-respect, grit,* and *healthy choices,* to name just a few examples, are words that have lost much of their power with youth. They are words that adults use when lecturing youth—so it's easy for students to tune them out. When these words do come up, immediately ask your students, "What does that word mean to you? What do you think it means to me? Imagine that word is a person walking down the hallway. What would that person look like? How would that person walk?" The goal is to have students define these words concretely so they are meaningful to them.

Self-esteem is another concept that students routinely dismiss because many have endured ineffective self-esteem programs, and many know cruel people who behave as if they have high self-esteem. We define *self-esteem* in the words of educator Dr. JoAnn Deak: "connectedness, compassion, and competency in fairly equal measure." Our goal is to enable our students to feel like they can navigate difficult social problems while being true to themselves and morally courageous in their actions. Through this process, they will develop self-esteem as a byproduct of those three "Cs." Or another way to think about it is from Dr. Tom Nehmy, who uses the term *self-compassion* as a counter to "self-esteem." Self-compassion is about how you treat yourself in times of challenge—something that transfers to how you treat others as well (http://www.healthymindsprogram.com.au/school-program).

But we think one of the most watered-down words in schools now is the word *bullying.* That's why *Owning Up,* which technically is a bullying prevention program, doesn't use the term in the lesson plans. We know that may seem odd, but after working throughout the country in all kinds of schools, we have received enough feedback that we are confident that framing these issues under the umbrella of bullying prevention is ineffective.

Confidentiality and Disclosures

Establishing confidentiality and creating a safe space are essential for the program's overall success. But in a limited way, we also want students to be allowed to share what they learned with their peers, parents, and other adults in their lives. Let them know that it's okay to discuss things generally—what happened in class, topics that were addressed, how they felt about the information, and so forth—but that they need to leave out names and details. Explain that you expect confidentiality regarding what students say—what is said in the room stays in the room, and that includes not posting things on any form of social media.

Students may disclose painful personal experiences, such as bullying and forms of trauma. Inform your students that if someone discloses that they or someone else could be in imminent physical danger, you and the student together will decide to report the problem to another adult to ensure they get the right support (meaning you're not going to immediately leave after the class and tell the principal or counselor without their knowledge). If a student reveals something painful in class, respond by saying, "I'm so sorry that happened to you, and we may need to do something about that. So let's set up a time after our session to figure out the best next steps." Your goal is to affirm the class but not to let the student's experience hijack the class. If the student reports to you privately (or when you meet with the student who spoke publicly), respond by saying, "I'm so sorry that happened to you, and thank you for placing your trust in me. What can I do that will support you right now in getting the help you need?" Make sure to ask the student if they currently feel safe. If not, you must report the abuse to the appropriate authorities. If the student does feel safe, ask whether they have talked to a counselor, and if not, offer to give them referral recommendations to get help. When a student discloses past abuse during a session, respond by saying, "I am so sorry that happened to you. Thank you for trusting all of us enough to talk about it here." You may also consider asking the student if they feel comfortable asking the other students how it feels to hear about their peer's experience.

It is also possible that students may disclose information that may not be accurate or true. When this happens, realize that these students are indicating that they have a problem (whether or not it is the problem they present) and that they still need help. Don't dismiss, or let others dismiss, the student as "just needing attention." It's a great opportunity to connect this dynamic back to the overall concept that dignity is not negotiable. As an educator, you should not be afraid of or intimidated by a disclosure—after all, you have created a safe environment where such disclosures can take place.

Snitching Versus Reporting

Some students may feel conflicted about whether or not to help themselves or a friend when they're in trouble for fear that they'll be seen as a snitch. Tell your students that *Owning Up* may help them think through how to report a problem and to know the difference between "snitching" and reporting. Reporting has the best interests of the other person in mind and involves telling a trusted adult so the adult can help solve a problem that is bigger than you. Its goal is to right a wrong. Snitching, on the other hand, is not about helping; rather, it is telling on someone with the intention of getting that person in trouble. A person reports a problem with the intention of making it go away, while a person snitches with the intention of making someone's problems bigger or more public.

Family

Understandably, parents can be curious about what will be taught in *Owning Up*. We are including a letter of introduction to parents and guardians for your use on page 145. It is critical to emphasize that parents and guardians should be informed of the general themes and goals of *Owning Up*. We want them to be part of the process. To that end, we believe the following is most important to communicate to the other adults in our students' lives:

1. We encourage students to discuss the themes we cover in the sessions with their parents and guardians.

2. We ask the students to respect the confidentiality of other students when they are telling another adult something about the session.

3. *Owning Up* educators are sensitive to the maturity level of the specific groups with which they work. *Owning Up* educators will not put words in their students' mouths.

4. If the parent, guardian, or another teacher has questions about the class, they are encouraged to speak with the *Owning Up* educator—we think there are countless opportunities to work together and reinforce positive messages to the young people in our lives.

Discipline

Owning Up educators are in some way teaching a class, so inevitably keeping the group on track is critical. When students are talking over one another, some effective methods we use have been just to stop talking, wait for students to realize that you are waiting for them to get themselves focused, say "everyone focus on me" and then begin again. Try not to say, "Shhhh . . . everyone be quiet" or "Settle down, everyone—remember, only one person at a time," or anything else teachers say that students regularly blow off. As a last resort, in the rare situation in which there is a group that is consistently disrespectful, we suggest you address them by saying, "In our guidelines, you asked me not treat you like you are 5 years old, but frankly, you are acting like a 5-year-old. I'm not enjoying being here with you. I love what I do, and I would like to be here with you, but not in this way."

A note about fidgeting: Some students may need to doodle or hold something in order to think and speak clearly. Fidgeting is not a discipline issue if it's not distracting the other students. This is especially true for young adolescents, who are growing rapidly and need to exert physical energy throughout the day. Rather than fight against this, find solutions. Allow students to doodle during discussions, and if you have a pen-tapper, let them tap on a mouse pad or other soft surface.

Being Challenged by a Student

What do you do if one of your students disrupts the group or challenges you as the educator? This student will often challenge your authority in front of other students, who will watch for your response. This challenge will likely come across in one of three ways. The first involves a student who slouches in the back with complete indifference but still manages to suck up all the energy. The second is when a student directly challenges you by being disrespectful to you or the other students. The third, and sometimes the most difficult, is when a student acts as though he or she is your peer.

In all three situations, you should respond by establishing your authority as the educator without humiliating or "powering over" the student who is challenging you. This situation presents an opportunity to demonstrate the curriculum in action. Arrange to meet with the student after the session. Make it clear that you respect the student but will not tolerate their behavior—be specific about the unacceptable behavior and its consequences. Acknowledge the student's position of power among his or her peers and reaffirm that you want the student in the group. If the behavior does not stop, make it clear that the student will have to leave. Depending on the severity of the problem, you may also choose to meet with the other members of the group. Depending on when you meet with them, you may have already covered the group dynamics session. If so, you can use that as a foundation for discussing the student's role in the group, and how their behavior is going against the class guidelines and what you want as a valued participant.

Maybe most challenging is preparing for the possibility that a student says something that is personally offensive to you or the other students. On one hand, *Owning Up* is about affirming every young person's right to "speak their truth." On the other hand, what happens if a student says a negative generalization based on race, class, gender orientation, sexual orientation, etc.? Your responsibility is to respectfully reaffirm the norms of the program that challenge these generalizations.

The Pack

A group of students may challenge your authority by turning their chairs away, talking to each other, or bullying other students in the group. Immediately separate these students by moving them apart in the room. If the pack of students continues to be disruptive, you might identify the leader and meet with this student after the session to articulate your requirements for continued participation in the group. After listening to what the student has to say about the situation, name the behavior you object to and establish the goals you want to accomplish by meeting. Find out why the student is responding in that way and what the student wants from the program. You can then work together to write up a contract outlining what the student needs to do to return. The goal of the meeting is twofold: to communicate that you respect the student and want the student to be in the program, and to indicate that the current behavior must change as you have requested for the student to continue to participate. With the remainder of the pack, depending on the group dynamics, you can meet with them individually or in a group to articulate your expectations. With any and all of the students involved, it's essential to take steps to reconnect the relationships. So when you confront students about a negative behavior in a session, the next time you meet them you need to reach out to them in a positive way.

Maturity and Experience Level

Your students will demonstrate a wide range of physical and emotional maturity. This dynamic can create a high degree of tension among students and may cause personal anxiety for students who worry if and how they fit in. Know that physical maturity can be a determinant of social status and individual placement in the social hierarchy. Sometimes students who are more physically or emotionally mature may have higher social status and power within the group. These students may, as a result, tend to dominate the discussion. At the other extreme, some physically mature students feel extremely uncomfortable with their bodies and will try to disappear into their clothes. As the educator, you need to be aware of these possible responses and incorporate this awareness into your strategy for creating opportunities for all students' participation.

Getting Stuck

It's normal to get stuck sometimes while conducting the sessions. It's also normal for students to be defensive, shut down, claim that "these things don't happen at our school—we have our groups, but we're not mean," or believe that there's no hope in changing the problems they experience or see in their schools and communities. When faced with this challenging dynamic, we recommend that you give each student a sheet of paper and a pencil and let them sit by themselves wherever they want in the room (except near a close friend). Ask them to write, anonymously, about whether the students who voice these opinions reflect their own experiences and beliefs. Give them 5 to 10 minutes to answer, then collect the papers. Next, have all the students sit in a circle and look at the floor, not touching each other. Read their responses aloud, and then ask the students what it felt like to hear their peers' answers. In doing this exercise, you have two goals: The first is to break the class dynamic in which some students silence other students. The second is to give students a firsthand experience of what happens when some students speak for others, and promote the idea that each person's truth is equally valid.

The *Owning Up* Community: You're Not Alone

No matter how much information we include on perceived challenges you might face while teaching *Owning Up*, we can't include everything. It could be a problem you experience teaching an activity, getting buy-in from colleagues and parents, or even logistical obstacles. Challenges like these can derail programs and undermine an educator's confidence and enthusiasm.

We believe great educators rely on reciprocal relationships with their colleagues. To that end, we have created the *Owning Up* Community to connect and encourage all of us to do our best work. We do not strive for uniformity but for unity because collaboration makes us stronger. The *Owning Up* Community will do this in the following ways:

- **Skill Sharing:** Share your favorite teaching tricks/tips/skills and tools with your friends and colleagues in friendly, no-pressure workalongs.

- **Coworking:** Get together to work on *Owning Up* lessons, help each other out, and share your work.

- **Build Community:** Meet new people in your field, organization, or community—and find out what we can do when we work together.

- **Join Us:** Use *Owning Up Online* to get help, talk about events, and share files.

We share ideas, meet with colleagues, and build community through the *Owning Up* Community. Join us there (www.owningup.online).

Assessment

Assessing the program is an important part of the *Owning Up Curriculum* and plays a role in building community support, orienting community members and program educators, determining program effectiveness, and gauging student participation and learning.

To begin the program we have given you a series of questions as a "Community Assessment" tool to help you set the priorities for the program. We encourage you to do the Community Assessment (page 19) with all the people responsible for scheduling, supporting, and implementing *Owning Up*. You don't have to answer all the questions, but still brainstorm together about the answers and why you are doing *Owning Up*. Creating community goals is critical. A second list of questions follows (page 20) and is directed at the individual educators who will be teaching *Owning Up*.

Measuring Program Effectiveness

To evaluate the impact of the curriculum in your own setting, you can use the *Owning Up* pretest/posttest, included as Appendix A. Administer the evaluation to students before beginning the program as a pretest and then as soon as possible after the conclusion of the program as a posttest. A comparison between the pretest and posttest results may help you gauge general changes or trends in students' attitudes as a result of their experience in the program.

It is also important to understand that the results of the surveys may vary depending on how many and which sessions you conduct. If possible, you should customize the surveys so that the questions reflect only the session content you intend to teach. You can also add questions about program logistics or how the educator conducted the sessions, if such feedback is desired.

Communicating With Families

Appendices B through D provide materials helpful for school administrators in establishing social justice and communicating with families. The following items are meant as a starting place for developing more detailed plans to improve the school climate:

- Starting the School Year Right: How Do We Address Bullying at Our School?
- Letter to Parent or Guardian of a Child Who Is Bullying
- Letter From Parent or Guardian Whose Child Is Being Bullied

Organizing the Sessions

Owning Up is designed to be taught on its own or integrated into a preexisting program. When it's taught on its own, as in a social studies or health class, it's usually taught once per week. If it's taught in an advisory capacity, one session can cover multiple advisories.

Group Composition

Group size is best between 10 and 25 students, but the sessions have been successfully taught with fewer or more students. The sessions have also been conducted with different grades together; however, we believe you have to be strategic about how you do that. For example, teaching sixth graders with eighth graders isn't ideal because it's just too hard to be appropriate for the sixth graders while being realistic for the eighth graders. Let's get even more specific: Imagine teaching a class that covers this content with eighth-grade girls in the same room as sixth-grade boys. It's fair to say that those groups of people live in two different worlds.

Session Length

The time it takes to conduct each *Owning Up Curriculum* session generally ranges from 45 minutes to an hour and 20 minutes. Because we include several different types of activities in every session, many of the sessions would appear to take far longer to complete. Our belief is that you need the option to select various activities for different types of learners (auditory, visual, and kinesthetic, for example). And we don't think anyone, no matter their age or gender, learns most effectively by sitting in a chair throughout a class listening to someone lecture at them.

Observers

If you are interested in having observers attend a session, or if people ask to attend, our suggestion is to limit it to two individuals, who sit at a distance from students. In addition, if you use another teacher's classroom and that person chooses to stay in the room (to observe, catch up on grading, etc.), it is of critical importance to articulate clear guidelines and expectations for that person before sessions begin. Specifically, if that teacher's presence makes the students unlikely to speak freely, the teacher should leave or you should find an alternative space.

Materials and Media

Materials necessary to run the program are readily available in most schools and organizational settings. These include a board or flip chart, drawing paper and markers, writing paper and pens or pencils, and a computer with internet access. We also occasionally encourage students to use their own technology throughout the program to blog or search for information related to the topic. Educators in school-based settings should check the technology-use and video guidelines for the school and school system before asking students to engage with their own devices.

At various points in the sessions, students are also invited to write about the issues that have been raised. In addition to these structured opportunities, we encourage using journals throughout the program, however long the program runs. We encourage you to seek out videos that interest your own group to reinforce the curriculum's themes and stimulate discussion. You can refer to our website (www.owningup.online), where we will continue to provide recommendations for timely material.

Using Art

We encourage you to use art—drawing, spoken word, or music—with your students, and we've included activities within the sessions you can use. Just be mindful about interpreting a student's artwork without his or her input, and to protect their art as if it is an extension of the student's body. If it's something they've made, ask for their permission before displaying it or sharing it with others, handle it with care, and store it in a safe place.

Conclusion

Owning Up addresses extremely challenging issues in our society. While we all want our students to be safe and healthy, creating strategies that truly enable this to happen takes moral courage, perseverance, and commitment. As an individual responsible for the implementation of *Owning Up,* you are the cornerstone for its success in your community. You are teaching your students to treat themselves and others with dignity. You are teaching them to educate themselves about power and privilege, oppression, personal accountability, and bearing witness when others oppress and discriminate against those who have less power. You are empowering them to work as agents of positive change and influence in their lives and in the lives of others—and we have the utmost confidence that you will do a great job.

For additional materials, including handouts and links to other resources, please visit our website: www.owningup.online

Community Assessment Questions

- What are the first words that come to mind when describing your community?

- What are the first words that come to mind when describing your students?

- How would parents, coaches, teachers, school staff, and students answer that question?

- Are there hallways, bathrooms, or other places in the school that students perceive as being "owned" by a particular group of students?

- Are there hallways, bathrooms, and other locations in the school where some students do not feel safe?

- Which school disciplinary procedures do students consider a slap on the wrist and which do they take seriously? Why?

- How does your school or institution assess if parents of different demographic groups feel comfortable reporting problems to authority figures?

- What are the mechanisms for reporting social cruelty, bullying, or violence in your school or organization? What are the strengths and weaknesses of this process?

- Have you asked students and adults in your setting how they feel about reporting procedures? For the students who have used them, do they describe the experience as being helpful or leading to more isolation?

- How are students given ownership of creating a culture of dignity in your school or organization?

Leader Assessment Questions

- What were you teased about in middle school or high school? How did you respond?

- Did another child or an adult intimidate you when you were young? Did you ask for help? From whom? What was the result?

- What group, if any, were you a part of during middle or high school?

- Who was your first crush? How did you feel when you saw that person? Did you ever tell that person you were interested?

- When you were growing up, what got respect and high social status as a boy or young man in your community?

- What got respect and high social status as a girl or young woman?

- Who was the best teacher or coach you had as a teen? Why?

- Who was the worst teacher or coach you had as a teen? Why?

- How do all these experiences influence the way you work with youth and adults in your community now?

- What characteristics do you have that would discourage any student from approaching you when they need help?

- What characteristics do you have that would encourage any student to approach you when they need help?

Getting Started

And (Hopefully) Not Wasting Your Time

SESSION 1

The main goal of the *Owning Up Curriculum* is to help students "own up," or take responsibility for and control of the decisions they make in life. This is hard to do no matter how old you are, but this curriculum is designed for young people between the ages of 11 and 14: individuals who are in an amazing, tumultuous, and intense time of life. *Owning Up* asks them to take a big risk—to be self-reflective and honest about participating in social dynamics that can demean and isolate people. Furthermore, *Owning Up* asks young people to take this risk in the presence of their peers.

Wherever you teach, as the educator, your responsibility is to create a safe, supportive, and inclusive environment where this risk taking is possible. Students have to believe in the process; they have to see that everyone in the group will be asked to examine and reflect on their own experiences—including the adults. That requires a foundation of mutual trust and respect between the educator and the students, as well as among the students themselves.

OBJECTIVES

- To establish program guidelines for educators and students
- To create the foundation for mutual trust where students will want to be self-reflective, engage with the group, and speak their truth
- To present the core concept that each individual's personal authenticity is connected to their right to be treated with dignity and the responsibility to treat others in the same manner
- To understand the positives and negatives of developing a personal armor

MATERIALS

- Whiteboard or flip chart
- Pencils or markers
- Approximately (ideally) 20 tennis balls, based on 25 students

Session Outline
What Are We Doing Today?

This session begins to create a safe environment for the students; it also lays the groundwork and sets the tone for the sessions that follow. Use the educator plan presented here and the following sessions as a guideline for expressing the main points (it's not a script to follow word for word), and be willing to go with the flow to respond to your students' questions, concerns, and views.

ACTIVITY: Cross Your Arms

Time: 5 minutes

Purpose: To put students in an "uncomfortable" situation

1. *Ask students to cross their arms.*
2. *Ask students to uncross their arms and let their hands hang free for a moment.*
3. *Ask students to cross their arms in the opposite direction.*
4. *Once they figure out how to do that, ask them to drop their hands again.*

Debrief

How uncomfortable did you feel with your arms crossed in the opposite position? It probably feels a lot less "normal" or comfortable that way. That's what this program (the time we spend together) may feel like: putting yourself in uncomfortable situations.

Takeaways

You cross your arms in the same way most of the time, but that doesn't make it "right"—it just makes it what you're used to. This program is about challenging you to figure out what you're used to and why, to allow yourself to feel uncomfortable, and then possibly to see things in a different way.

ACTIVITY: Silent Passing

Time: 10 minutes

Purpose: To teach students that communication gets progressively more difficult the more balls they have in the air

1. *Separate students into groups of at least five but no more than eight.*
2. *Hand out one ball per group.*
3. *Silently toss the ball among all the people in the group.*

4. *Gradually add more balls until each group has members tossing four or five balls to each other simultaneously.*

5. *Say:* If you drop a ball or throw a bad pass, you remove yourself from the group.

6. *Tell students they can rejoin the group, but don't specify how.*

7. *Stop the game after several minutes of students stepping in and out of their circle.*

Debrief

- Why do you think we played this game?

- How did it feel trying to get back into the group?

- How did it feel not knowing how to get back in or when?

- What are the different ways people tried to communicate with each other? Did it work?

Takeaways

- It's easy to communicate when there is only one ball in the air, and it gets more difficult with each additional ball.

- When each group had one ball, they were able to manage it all together. But when you're juggling a lot (which all of you are), it gets a lot more difficult.

- Everyone in this room is probably juggling lots of balls in the air. *Owning Up* will teach you how to communicate better with other people—especially when you get frustrated or annoyed at something they're doing.

ACTIVITY: Creating Group Guidelines

Time: 15 minutes

Purpose: To establish session guidelines

Before we move on, we need to set up some guidelines for our group. The first part of doing this is describing what you need from me so you walk out of every session feeling like you've gotten something out of it and I haven't wasted your time. I also want you to tell me about anything in general that would make you not want to participate.

Write students' responses down on the whiteboard or flip chart.

- What guidelines and expectations should I follow when we meet? (Listen, don't lecture, don't yell, don't talk down to us.)

- What guidelines and expectations should you have for yourselves? (Be honest, listen to each other, respect each other, own up to your actions.)

- Assume people have the best intentions.

- If you're offended by something someone says, ask for clarification of what they meant.

- Before passing judgment on someone, gather more information.

- What guidelines should I have for you? (Tell me what you truly think, not what you think I want to hear. Let me know if you can't relate to the topics we cover.)

If students say, "Respect each other," ask them to give concrete examples of respect. Examples could be, You speak for yourself, not others; you don't roll your eyes; you don't say, "No offense, but . . ."

> Here's a guideline you can share with your students as well: "It's possible I may struggle with some of the things we talk about. I may really disagree with something I hear in class. When that happens, it may be hard for me, so I will be learning with you. But we will stick with the idea of everyone deserving to be treated with dignity, and that should get us through some of these tougher topics."

ACTIVITY: Understanding Confidentiality

THINK ABOUT IT

Time: 5 minutes

Purpose: To reaffirm the definition of *confidentiality* for the students

The group's guidelines create a safe space for owning up by establishing trust, honesty, and willingness to listen for all participating students and leaders. You are encouraged to use your own words, phrases, and language to talk about the issues and topics.

Some of these terms could be considered "bad words" that you usually wouldn't say in an educational environment. But if you use these words in context, as part of a point you want to make, then you are encouraged to use them.

There is also a possibility that people in the group might say the "right" things but then behave the opposite way as soon as they leave the room. This doesn't mean the group isn't working. It means that what we are trying to accomplish is hard and doesn't happen overnight. Observe what's happening and ask yourself why the person is choosing to act the way they are (and that includes you if you find yourself in the same situation).

If you feel strongly that there is a big contradiction between what is being said in this group and how people are behaving outside the group (and you may already expect that to happen), you can come to me privately and share your thoughts.

The guidelines for the group also include that while you can share generally what we discuss in our sessions, what is specifically said in the room stays in the room. However, please know that if someone discloses that they or someone else are in imminent danger, then I'm going to work with that student to find another adult who can help. If a situation like this should happen, I won't tell another adult without your knowledge. We will work together to choose the person you feel most comfortable going to, and I will do my best to maintain your privacy.

Debrief

- *Owning Up* is what you learn in school that's not taught in books. It's about what happens in the hallways, in the lunchroom, in your classes. It's about the unwritten rules that may direct your or your peers' opinions and actions.

- You can expect that there will be moments in this program you won't like. Either you'll really disagree with something someone has said, or you won't like what we are discussing.

- If that happens, ask yourself why you are having that reaction, think about it, and then state your opinion.

Takeaways

- As the adult running these sessions, I don't assume I know what is going on in your life. I will present you with information. All I ask of you is to engage with the group and participate, even if—and especially if—you disagree.

- If you aren't getting what you need from this program, or any program like it, ask for what you need. You owe that to yourself and your education.

- This program will present you with one way to look at the world. Not everyone sees things in the same way. But our time together is grounded on the belief that your dignity, your worth, and the dignity of others are nonnegotiable. The goal of the program is to help you understand what is behind common yet difficult problems many people experience and to give you concrete, realistic solutions. Before we go on, let's take a few moments to be clear about definitions.

ACTIVITY: Getting Clear About Words

Time: 5 minutes

Purpose: To clarify definitions of *dignity* and *respect*

People can use words assuming that the person they're speaking to agrees with what the terms mean. So before we go on, let's make sure we agree about some terms.

What does *dignity* mean? It comes from the Latin word *dignitas,* which means "to be worthy." Dignity is a given. What does *respect* mean? It comes from the Latin word *respectus,* which means "to look back at." Today, respect is defined as "a feeling of deep admiration for someone or something elicited by their abilities, qualities, or achievements." Unlike dignity, which each person gets no matter what, respect is earned.

Debrief/Takeaways

- What's your personal definition of *dignity?* What images, sounds, colors, etc., come to mind when you hear/see the word *dignity*?

- What's your personal definition of *respect?* What images, sounds, colors, etc., come to mind when you hear/see the word *respect*?

ACTIVITY: No Assumptions

Time: 15 minutes

Purpose: To create a safe space for students to share their experiences

We don't want to make any assumptions about anyone in this room. So we are going to do a quick activity that will give us some knowledge about people's experiences without calling anyone out. Take out a piece of paper and a pencil or pen. I am going to read aloud the following statements. Every time I say something that you have experienced, write down a slash or a tally. If you're worried about people looking at which ones you mark, feel free to cover your paper with your other hand. After I read all the statements I am going to collect all the papers, total the marks, and then divide by the number of students in the room to get the class average. Or we can do the math together. It's your choice.

Here are the statements:

1. I have not been invited to something I really wanted to go to.
2. I have been unfairly labeled.
3. People have talked behind my back or gossiped about me.
4. I have pretended to be more confident than I really am.
5. I have not been able to talk to a friend about something important to me because I was worried they'd laugh at me or use it against me.
6. I have heard bad gossip about someone else.
7. I have been rejected by someone I really liked.
8. I have been caught up in a drama I wanted nothing to do with.
9. A friend made fun of me about something painful and didn't stop even though they knew I hated it.
10. I've been so angry I wanted to explode, but I didn't say anything.
11. My parents are divorced or not together.
12. I've been teased about the way I look.
13. I have dreaded going to school.
14. I've been at school pretending to be fine when I'm really not.

Debrief

- How does it feel even to write down those marks?
- How does it feel to know there are other people here who may have answered yes to the same statements as you?
- How are you feeling right now?

Takeaways

- People in this room have had similar experiences.
- You are not alone if you have struggled with a problem.

ACTIVITY: Building Our Armor

Time: 15 minutes

Purpose: To process and put into words how students "choose" to present themselves in public versus how they may really be feeling

We just admitted that sometimes we go to school pretending we're fine when we really aren't. How do we do this? Maybe one way of thinking about it is everyone has their own personal armor they wear to get through their day.

Give each student a piece of 12" by 18" paper with a drawing of a person wearing armor.

Draw in pictures and/or words what you show people on the outside. On the back of the paper write what you don't show people, and if you would like to share it with the group or not.

Debrief

- In general, what are the positives of wearing this armor?
- In general, what are the negatives of wearing this armor?
- What are the positives and negatives of the particular armor you wear, and why did you choose it? Would you rather change it for something else? When do you take it off?
- Was your armor made overnight, or was it made over time?
- What would happen if you showed the parts of yourself you usually keep hidden?

Takeaways

- Everybody wears some form of armor.
- Some share what's underneath; others keep it completely hidden.
- There can be really good reasons why people hide parts of themselves or how they're feeling. Other times, hiding feelings can make problems feel overwhelming. We will examine both throughout our time together.

Wrap It Up

Time: 5 minutes

Everyone in this room has gone through challenging experiences:

- Some of you have gone through similar experiences.
- When you see someone act a certain way they may be feeling differently than you would assume.

Carry It With You

Let's choose a few times during a normal day when you can try to remember to check in with yourself.

- Can you feel it when you walk into your school? When does the armor come on? Can you visualize what it looks like?
- What does it feel like walking between classes? During lunch?
- Observe other people. Can you see their armor?

Getting Out of the Box

SESSION
2

Are We Boxed Into Gender Norms?

Whether you teach *Owning Up* in a single-gender or mixed-gender group, our students have to work, cooperate, and be in relationships with one another. As described in the "Getting Started" section, our students live in a world that is highly separated by strict gender norms, while at the same time many of those norms are being openly challenged—often by our own students. This dynamic doesn't diminish the importance of educating our children about how gender norms influence people's behavior, self-identity, and self-esteem. Indeed, it makes it even more important.

Owning Up does this throughout the sessions, but this session teaches it most explicitly by using the Act Like a Girl and Act Like a Boy Boxes. These modules are incredible teaching tools to explain privilege of any kind (gender, race, class, etc.), but the lesson objective may be too abstract for your less mature, more concrete thinkers. In our experience, the Box exercises should not be taught to sixth graders because they can interpret them as either a blueprint for achieving high social status or a framework for shame if they identify as being "outside the box." However, for more mature students (some seventh graders and the majority of eighth graders), this exercise will be a touchstone you can use throughout all the sessions you teach.

OBJECTIVES

- To identify how gender socialization influences personal development
- To identify how social norms and rules can influence perception
- To link those rules to how students are conditioned to accept or be silent bystanders to discrimination in many forms
- To empower students to challenge these rules and develop a more authentic self-identity and voice

MATERIALS

- Whiteboard or flip chart
- Index cards
- Markers
- *Optional:* Video of your choice and equipment to show it

Session Outline

What Are We Doing Today?

We are learning about an invisible set of rules that often guides and can even control people's feelings and behavior.

Review It

Time: 10 minutes

Purpose: To have students remember their guidelines and share what they observed since the last session

Last session we talked about a lot of things, but let's start off with the guidelines you came up with. If you look on the board, you can see that I've written "Guidelines for Me" and "Guidelines for Each Other" on two areas of the board. Please write down the guidelines you remember that you want me to follow and the guidelines you want all of us to follow.

Now that we remember our guidelines, I want to know about the Carry It With You activity I asked you to do. Remember we talked about people walking around with their own kinds of armor? We agreed to observe ourselves and others at specific times of day. To get started, let's share our observations.

- Can you describe what you saw or felt at school?
- Walking into school?
- Walking between class periods?
- During recess or lunch?
- Do you have other insights and/or things you thought about from the last session?

ACTIVITY: Being Boxed In

THINK ABOUT IT

Time: 30 minutes

Purpose: To enable students to visualize gender normalization and privilege

Say: Why do we have rules? Has anyone made you follow a rule you didn't like? How about a rule you hated or that made no sense to you? Can you give some examples?

Now we are going to talk about an invisible set of rules that often guides and can even control people's feelings and behavior. It's a little weird, though, because you can't see it—but it's there. It's called the Act Like a Girl Box and Act Like a Boy Box.

Let's start with some examples.

Girls: Have you experienced boys doing things you really don't understand or that frustrate you? Let's put down examples for each:

> Are way too loud
>
> Act perverted
>
> Do gross things
>
> Treat you much nicer one-on-one than when you are around him and his friends

Boys: Have you experienced girls doing things you really don't understand or that frustrate you? Let's put down examples for each:

> Go to the bathroom in groups or "huge herds"
>
> Scream in the hallway
>
> Talk really fast
>
> Say they're not mad at you when they really are

Let's go over the definition of two words: *society* and *culture.*

> **Society:** People living together in a more or less ordered community.
>
> **Culture:** A set of beliefs, customs, and social norms shared by a specific group of people.
>
> ***Owning Up* definition of culture:** Everything we "know" but have never been officially taught.

Now I'm going to ask you two questions. I want you to be as specific as possible in your answers. For example, if one of your answers is "sports," I want you to be specific about what kind of sport you're thinking of. The first question is:

- *For the girls:* What are the characteristics society (or our culture) wants girls to have?
- *For the boys:* What are the characteristics society (or our culture) wants boys to have?

Write their responses in two columns in the center of the board or flip-chart paper.

The second question is:

- *For the girls:* What are the characteristics society doesn't want girls to have?
- *For the boys:* What are the characteristics society doesn't want boys to have?

Write these responses around the words you first wrote. Finally, draw a box around the first set of words, as the sample diagram shows.

- Where do these messages come from? Who is saying them to you?
- How much do you think these boxes affect the adults in your school?
- How much do you think these boxes affect the students in your school?

Act Like a Girl

Overweight

Bad skin

Tries too hard

Clingy

Pretty

People know you

Thin but with the right curves

Good/nice hair

Athletic but not too big

Confident

Right style/tech

Smart but doesn't freak
out about grades

Boys like her

Overreacts

Acts/looks too
much like a guy

Less money
compared
to others

"Too" aggressive

Act Like a Boy

Disabilities

Awkward

Snitch

Bad style/tech

Funny

Tall

Strong

Confident

Good at sports

Good style/tech

Good at comebacks

Doesn't take anything too seriously

Knows how to talk to girls

Acts like a girl

Easily upset or
bothered

Gay

Less money
compared to
others

Debrief/Takeaways

Say: It's really hard to do this exercise and not think about where you fit or don't fit in the box. It's really hard to do this exercise and not think about where other people fit. And it's really hard to do this exercise and not compare yourself to other people. But that's not what this exercise is about. Instead, this exercise is about showing how sometimes people have power and influence over others. It's about how we can be influenced by these invisible rules so that we think if we have the highest number of things in the box, we will be happy.

The boxes also try to convince you that it's not worth challenging the people who have power. The boxes teach a negative form of loyalty—where even if you think something is wrong you don't say anything because loyalty in the boxes means being silent or joining in when someone with more power is being mean to someone with less power.

Throughout our sessions, we will refer to these boxes to understand people's motivations and actions.

No matter what we think about the box, we all are influenced by it to some extent. For example, a girl really may not care about conforming to what's inside the box at her school; however, she is still interacting with boys and girls at her school who do.

People who look like they are in the middle of the box may not like being there. They may feel pressure to uphold a certain reputation or to maintain their image.

Some of the characteristics inside and outside the boxes are just things people currently have or are dealing with—they can't help it. Either way, they shouldn't be judged for something about themselves that they can't control.

ACTIVITY: Bystanding

Time: 10 minutes

Purpose: To explain the dynamics of bystanding

The box also explains how bystanding occurs—when someone doesn't do anything when someone else is being treated badly.

Debrief

Looking at the boxes, what do you think is the Act Like a Girl or Act Like a Boy definition?

- The box convinces bystanders to join the person being mean because they don't want to be pushed outside the box.

- Sometimes people don't want to get involved and may have really good reasons for their decision. To the target, however, that "neutral" behavior usually looks like siding with the person with more power (meaning they don't look neutral to the target).

- People often make the decision to intervene depending on how much they like, don't like, or even know the people involved.

Takeaways

The definition of *bystander* is a person who is present at an event but doesn't take part.

ACTIVITY: How Do These Rules Affect You?

Time: 20 minutes

Purpose: To challenge students to understand their school culture

Discussion questions (choose three or four that best fit your students). You may also use these as a personal-reflection writing exercise, with discussion to follow.

- What are the differences between the Act Like a Girl and Act Like a Boy Boxes?
- What are the similarities?
- Which box do you think has more rules?
- Does one have more power than the other?
- Do you think the boxes exist in your school? How?
- How do you think the box creates pressure for boys to act a certain way with their guy friends? With girls?
- How do you think the box creates pressure for girls to act a certain way with their girl friends? With guys?
- How do girls reinforce the Act Like a Boy Box for boys?
- How do boys reinforce the Act Like a Girl Box for girls?
- How would the box influence someone to make the decision to intervene in a conflict with other people?

ACTIVITY: Your Brain Development and the Box

Time: 10 minutes

Purpose: To have students make the connection that one of the reasons why they are feeling these comparisons so intensely is their brain development

When you go through puberty, amazing things happen in your brain. It's growing and changing, and important, incredible things are happening. One of the things that happens is that dopamine, a chemical in the brain that signals pleasure, is becoming increasingly active—think of it as your reward center. It's one of the reasons why you may feel things so intensely right now. It's one of the reasons why music may be so important to you, or why you may feel so strongly about your friendships. But there are complications to this increase in your reward centers. One of those complications is that it's common to be really driven to get praise and attention from your peers—and to be really sensitive to criticism and comparisons as well.

Debrief

Just knowing that there is something in your brain that makes you more sensitive to what other people think about you, or that drives your desire to have specific things, can be empowering.

Takeaways

You know where the desire is coming from: biologically, your brain is developing this way. But it's our culture, those invisible rules, that tells you what you should value or not. Can you think of an example?

ACTIVITY: Groups Take Apart the Boxes

Time: 15 minutes

Purpose: To make the connections among the boxes, school culture, and the problems middle school students commonly experience

Students form small groups and discuss how the Act Like a Girl and Act Like a Boy Boxes operate to control students' behavior, and what they can do to intervene in one or more of the following situations. To break up existing groups, you can have the students number off (all the 1s together, all the 2s, etc.). Choose one or two situations from the list below, and then have them discuss the two questions on the next page. Each group should have a recorder who writes down their thoughts and a reporter who is prepared to report back to the larger group.

Situation 1: Four girls are in a close group. As they pass another girl in the hall, one of the four makes a comment about the girl wearing something that looks really bad on her. Two of the other girls join in, making similar comments. The fourth girl laughs.

Situation 2: A star athlete hates playing because of all the pressure but won't quit.

Situation 3: A boy is obsessed with getting (*insert name of shoe*).

Situation 4: A guy is really struggling with his grades, even though he's trying, but he doesn't want to admit to anyone how bad he feels.

Situation 5: A girl dumps an old friend because her new friends tell her they don't like her.

Have a discussion with your students to understand their culture using the following questions:

> **Question 1:** How do you think your life would change if people you know weren't so influenced by the boxes?

> **Question 2:** What is one thing you can do to make Act Like a Girl or Act Like a Boy Boxes less powerful?

Reconvene and have the small groups share what they discussed. Each group contributes one answer to the two questions.

Wrap It Up

Time: 5 minutes

The box is a way of understanding people's behavior. It's not about where people fit. Rather, it's about looking at the world through a particular set of glasses so you can see things in a different way.

- The box can influence how you think about yourself and other people in ways that may not be good for you.
- If you feel uncomfortable about what we covered in the session today, just like any other session, come and talk to me about it.
- In your life, who are the people you respect the most? Often, people who are truly respected by others are not controlled by the box.

Carry It With You

- Watch your actions, thoughts, and feelings to see if the rules of the box are influencing you. You can also see if people around you are influenced by the box.
- If you catch yourself being guided by the box, break the specific rule you think the box is trying to make you follow.

Just Kidding

Why Are We Really Laughing?

SESSION
3

One of the more confusing yet common experiences for middle school students is how teasing is used to describe a wide variety of behaviors. It can be very frustrating for students because they feel like there is an expectation that teasing is harmless and if it bothers them, there's something wrong with them. This session clarifies the difference between harmless teasing and using that term as a cover to get away with hurting people.

OBJECTIVES

- To further understand the armor image and how it connects to unwritten rules of conduct for boys and girls
- To create a definition of *humor*
- To define good, annoying, and bad teasing
- To affirm that people are entitled to their own feelings and perceptions, and that no one gets to decide how someone else feels

MATERIALS

- Whiteboard or flip chart
- Three signs, reading *Strongly Agree, Agree With Both,* and *Strongly Disagree,* placed in areas of the room that are as far apart as possible
- Paper and pencils
- Index cards
- Masking tape

Session Outline

What Are We Doing Today?

We are learning about the different kinds of teasing and the positives and negatives of friendships.

Review It

Time: 10 minutes

Reproduce on the board the Act Like a Girl and Act Like a Boy Boxes the students created last class.

Say: Last session we talked about the Act Like a Girl and Act Like a Boy Boxes. Did anyone see any examples of the boxes influencing people?

ACTIVITY: Defining Friendships

Time: 15 minutes

Purpose: To identify the positives and negatives of friendships

Using the following questions, generate a discussion about friendship. Write students' responses on the board. Designate a recorder (to scribe the answers) and a reporter (to share the answers aloud) for each group. Then have each group generate a list of answers in response to the questions below and compile them as a group on the board.

You also can have each student answer the questions individually on index cards, and then compile them as a group on the board.

- Positive: What do you like about your friendships?
- Negative: What don't you like about your friendships?

If the students say jealousy, competitiveness, or being judgmental on the negative side, ask them what they are jealous, competitive, or judgmental about. You'll find that it's usually about the same things: looks, clothes, popularity, friends, and sometimes grades.

Debrief

Once they have created their positive and negative friendship lists, and you've written their responses on the board or flip chart, ask the following questions:

- What have you noticed about the list you made?
- Is there a pattern to either side of the list?
- What do you think about any patterns you noticed?

Takeaways

People have their own concepts of the positive and negative sides of friendship, but there are also patterns that they share.

ACTIVITY: What's Your Experience?

Time: 5 minutes

Purpose: To have students "own" their actions

Close your eyes (or put your head on the table) and raise your hand if you know someone who has done any of the things that are on the negative side of the list. Keep your hand up, open your eyes, and look around.

Close your eyes again and raise your hand if you yourself have done any of the things on the negative side of the list. Open your eyes and look around.

Debrief

- What did you learn, and what did you feel about doing that?
- What was the most uncomfortable part?
- What was the most surprising part?

Takeaways

Say: What we just did when you raised your hands is what this program is all about—"owning up." But it can be uncomfortable because it's usually way easier to focus on the things that happen to us than on what we do to other people.

ACTIVITY: Your Friendship Bill of Rights

Time: 10–15 minutes

Purpose: To have each student define the qualities of a good friend

I am going to give you your personal Friendship Bill of Rights (see Appendix E). On it, you'll find three questions for you to answer. The first asks you to identify what, for you, are the most important characteristics someone should have in order to be a good friend. The second asks you to state how someone would treat you were you not to consider that friendship particularly strong or dependable. The third question asks you to think about the quality of your friendships: Do they measure up to what you say you need? Are you treating people according to what you say you value in a friendship?

Debrief/Takeaways

What did you learn about yourself from doing this exercise?

ACTIVITY: Three Corners Exercise

Time: 10 minutes

Purpose: To allow students to move around and begin thinking about the topics being covered in today's session

I've made three signs: *Strongly Agree, Agree With Both,* and *Strongly Disagree.* Notice that I've placed them in areas of the room that are as far apart as possible.

I'm going to read statements aloud, and when I do, I want each of you to think about the statement and then walk, without talking, to the corner you agree with.

After reading each statement, give students a few moments to get to their corners. Then ask students at "their" corner to discuss their opinion among themselves. After a few minutes ask a student from each group to report what people in the group said.

Statements:

- People are always happy when they laugh.
- When someone says, "No offense, but . . ." they really don't want to hurt your feelings.
- Boys think all gross jokes or comments are funny.
- You shouldn't take things too seriously.

ACTIVITY: Is This Funny?

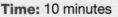
THINK ABOUT IT

Time: 10 minutes

Purpose: To break down misconceptions about why people laugh

The common assumption is that people laugh when they think something is funny. But are there other reasons why people laugh?

Examples:

- They're nervous.
- They're uncomfortable.
- They don't know what to say.

In addition, people have different ideas of what they think is funny. No one has the right to make someone feel stupid, sensitive, or weird if they don't think something is funny that you do. Let's make a list of general ideas of what is funny and what is not.

Funny	Not Funny
Tickling	Tickling
Fart jokes	Fart jokes
Talking about other people	Talking about other people
Cat videos	Cat videos
	Girls/periods (not ever funny)
	Things people can't control, like acne (not ever funny)

Debrief

Everyone has their own definition of what's funny, and all are valid, as long as they don't hurt someone else.

Takeaways

The problem is, it can be uncomfortable to tell people when you don't think something is funny because it could make things uncomfortable between you, or you could appear to take things too seriously.

ACTIVITY: Breaking Down Different Types of Teasing

Time: 15 minutes

Purpose: To define different types of teasing for students

THINK ABOUT IT

Humor, teasing each other, and joking around can be a sign that people are close friends. Humor can be a powerful tool to defend yourself against people who want to make fun of you. But teasing and humor can also be used to make someone feel bad, especially when people know specific things someone is sensitive about. Teasing can be really confusing for people. Sometimes you can't tell if people are really joking/teasing or if they are just pretending to be joking/teasing but really want to hurt your feelings. Even more confusing is when people say they're "just kidding," so they can be hurtful but get out of taking responsibility for their behavior and blame the person they're teasing for being too sensitive.

Let's break down the different kinds of teasing so it's easier to figure out what's going on.

Let's brainstorm examples of good teasing . . .

Good teasing—people enjoy the teasing

- You feel liked by the teaser—both people enjoy the teasing
- You don't feel the teaser's motivation is to put you down
- If you decide you don't like it, you can say something and it will stop
- Democracy of teasing—everyone in the group is able to tease and be teased

Let's brainstorm examples of annoying teasing . . .

> Annoying teasing—the teaser finds it more enjoyable than the person getting teased
>
> - You don't like it, and you feel the teaser should know you don't like it but somehow they don't
> - It makes you feel too sensitive or uptight (you can't take a joke)
> - It makes you feel frustrated
> - You are teased about the same thing over and over
> - You can say you don't like it, but the teaser laughs or ignores you

Let's brainstorm examples of malicious teasing . . .

> Malicious (bad) teasing—the teaser intentionally attempts to hurt the other person
>
> - You feel like the teasing is being done to put you down
> - You are being teased about things other people know make you uncomfortable
> - If you defend yourself, you are blamed for not being able to take a joke; the teasing gets much worse and the teaser brings other people into it
> - The teasing is relentless (it doesn't stop)
> - It's done in front of other people

Debrief

Usually there are three types of teasing: good teasing, annoying teasing, and malicious (bad) teasing.

Takeaways

People have their own concepts of what good teasing is. Some people are more sensitive than others, and it's really important to respect people's feelings. And everyone has the right to say when they think someone has gone over the line when teasing them or someone else.

Wrap It Up

> **Time:** 10 minutes

- Everyone has the right to have their feelings and opinions respected.
- But it can be really hard to say what they feel.
- Don't take advantage of other people feeling so embarrassed that they don't say what they feel.

Carry It With You

- See if you catch yourself saying, "Just kidding," "Just joking," or "No offense but . . ." between this session and the next. Then ask yourself why you said it. What type of teasing were you doing?
- See if you can identify someone in your life who uses humor well or knows how to respond when people try to put them down.

SEAL

I Know What the Problem Is, but How Do I Fix It?

In this session, students will learn the SEAL strategy for communicating in conflict or other difficult situations. SEAL is one of the fundamental social skills you will teach in this curriculum. Be sure to explain to your students that when using SEAL, getting through any of the steps is considered a success. It doesn't guarantee that other people will change their behavior, but it helps students increase their social skills to work through conflicts and feel more in control of the situation.

OBJECTIVES

- To present the SEAL strategy as a communication strategy
- To increase awareness of nonverbal communication
- To encourage students to begin practicing SEAL in their own lives
- To define the components of a sincere apology
- To define *listening* as being prepared to be changed by what you hear

MATERIALS

- Whiteboard or flip chart
- Index cards
- Paper, pencils, markers
- Tape—duct or drafting

Session Outline

What Are We Doing Today?

We are learning about how to deal with other people when we are frustrated, angry, or worried about them.

Review It

Time: 5–10 minutes

Ask:

- Did anyone experience a good teasing moment since our last session?
- Did you catch yourself saying, "Just kidding" or "No offense"?
- How did it feel the moment you caught yourself, and did you do anything different when you made that realization?

ACTIVITY: On the Line

Time: 10 minutes

Purpose: To let students move around and think about topics you will cover in today's session

Put a line of duct tape on the ground, with one end signifying to students that they strongly agree and the other that they strongly disagree. Tell students you are going to read aloud five statements and that they should place themselves on the line that most accurately reflects their opinion.

Statements:

- A guy can show his anger without being teased.
- It's hard to know when a girl is angry.
- It's hard to know when a guy is angry.
- People usually tell you when they are angry.
- When people apologize, they usually mean what they say.

After reading each statement, give students a few minutes to get to their spots. Then ask students at various spots on the line to explain why they feel the way they do. After the discussion, point out that whether students agree or disagree with the statements, they all have a right to their opinion.

ACTIVITY: What Does Anger Look Like to You?

Time: 15 minutes

Purpose: To have students describe the experience of being angry through writing, drawing, and/or music

When you carry anger around with you, what does it feel like in your body? What does it feel like when it's sitting in your mind?

Can you imagine where it's hanging out? What it's doing? If it were an animal, what would it look like? Draw what you imagine, and include any words to accompany it. You could also write a poem if you like. If you have a way to play music, choose a song that describes your feelings in this situation. But keep it appropriate, because remember: We are in class!

Debrief/Takeaways

Your feelings "sit" in your body, and somehow those feelings need to get out.

ACTIVITY: Rules of Anger

Time: 15 minutes

Purpose: To connect students' experiences with cultural constructs of expressing anger

Do you think boys and girls express their anger in the same way? Why or why not?

How do you see boys express their anger most often? *(Instructor note: Below are some suggestions.)*

- Keep their feelings inside
- Pretend it doesn't bother them
- Hold their feelings inside until something small makes them explode

How do you see girls express their anger most often? *(Instructor note: Below are some suggestions.)*

- Keep their feelings inside
- Get other people on their side
- Hold their feelings inside until something small makes them explode

Conduct a general discussion about anger, asking the following questions:

- Why do people hold in their anger for so long?
- What do you think happens to people who bottle up their anger?
- How can anger be productive?
- Can anger be used for good?

ACTIVITY: What Rule Were They Following?

Time: 15 minutes

Purpose: To link the rules of anger to common situations

Ask students to think about the following situations in connection to the rules of anger; people's personal armor that we discussed in the first session (or the Act Like a Girl/Act Like a Boy Boxes, if you have taught them); and how they influence people's interactions when they're in conflict with one another:

1. A friend is mad at you but won't admit it to your face.
2. You're mad at a friend, so you give them small hints about how you feel.
3. A friend is telling you why he hates this other person. You don't agree 100%, but you say you agree with your friend.
4. One friend is mad at another friend and drags everyone else into the problem. Then everyone take sides.
5. For no apparent reason, a kid on your team punches a locker after practice.

Debrief

What rule was guiding the person's actions in each situation?

Takeaways

Once you are aware of how these rules can guide your actions, it's easier to take a step back and be more in control of yourself.

ACTIVITY: Understanding SEAL

Time: 15 minutes

Purpose: To teach the SEAL strategy

Say: At some point, everyone has misunderstandings and conflicts with others. SEAL is our strategy for communicating when you're angry at, frustrated with, or even worried about someone. I know that ideas like this can seem really weird, immature, or unrealistic, and I don't want you to sound like a robot. So SEAL is never going to tell you what to say. SEAL is going to give you a way to think through stressful conflicts with other people. Using SEAL doesn't make the problem go away, but hopefully it can give you some power in the situation and improve your chances of being taken seriously.

SEAL is also about identifying what people could say in response, the "pushback" that would make it more difficult for you to achieve your goals because whatever they say in their pushback makes you so angry, defensive, or annoyed that you lose control of yourself. (Being angry is never pleasant, but using SEAL channels your anger in a productive way.)

Explain that SEAL is an acronym for the steps in the strategy. Write the steps on the board or flip chart, then discuss what each step means.

Stop: Breathe, observe, and ask yourself what the situation is about. Decide when and where you can talk to the person so the person will be most likely to listen to you.

Explain: Take your bad feelings and put them into words—be specific about what you don't like and what you want to happen instead. You realize you are making a request, so you know you may not get what you want. But at least you are being clear with yourself and others.

Affirm and acknowledge: State your right to be treated with dignity by the other person, and your responsibility to do the same in return. If appropriate, acknowledge your part in contributing to the situation.

Lock:

- *Lock in the friendship:* Decide to make the friendship stronger by talking about the problem.
- *Take a break:* Decide to take a break from the friendship but agree to talk later about reestablishing the friendship.
- *Lock out the friendship:* As a last resort, when you really feel that your feelings and personal boundaries aren't being respected, decide to end the friendship.

If students are struggling with the "Lock" part of SEAL, good questions to ask them are "When is it okay to decide not to be friends?" "Will this be a difficult process?" and "Do you have any examples of situations like this?" We want young people to face these difficult moments and understand that friendships are stronger when people work through difficult feelings. But we also want them to recognize the signs that they are in an unhealthy or unsafe friendship right now—and to set a good foundation for other relationships when they are older.

ACTIVITY: Applying SEAL

Time: 20 minutes

Purpose: To apply SEAL to scenarios students can relate to and have them analyze the process

Read the following scenarios aloud to the group. You can either decide which one to do or ask your students which is most appropriate for them. Or they can come up with a scenario of their own. For each scenario, guide the exercise by having students first act out what the characters would usually do and then act out the situation again using SEAL to frame their words.

Scenario 1: Naomi is friends with Caitlin, but Naomi hates how Caitlin makes fun of her and then says "I'm just joking!" Naomi has never told Caitlin how she feels.

Scenario 2: Jason is in (*your students' grade*). Two of his close friends, Carl and Shawn, think it's really funny to tease him all the time. Usually, Jason pretends he's fine with how they mess with him, but one day he blows up. After the blowup, Jason wants to talk to his friends because he wants them to stop, but he's embarrassed about his blowup.

Scenario 3: Laila's friends like playing a game at recess that she hates. They run away from her at recess or talk about things she doesn't know anything about. When she tells them she doesn't like what they're doing, they tell her to play with someone else.

Debrief/Takeaways

- The first time you acted out the scenario, when were the moments the problem got bigger or worse?

- If this happened in real life, what would the characters learn, both positive and negative, from the experience?

- The second time you acted out the scenario, how did the person using SEAL respond to the pushback?

- When was it most difficult to follow the SEAL strategy? Why?

- Do you have any suggestions for how we can make the SEAL strategy we saw more effective?

- What would effective bystanding look like in these situations?

- Should we try it again?

ACTIVITY: The Art of Apology

THINK ABOUT IT

Time: 10 minutes

Purpose: To define *apology*

At some point in your life, there will come a point when you'll have to apologize for something you did. Maybe you didn't mean it, maybe you didn't realize what you did, or maybe you did know what you were doing. When you acknowledge that you have hurt someone and show that acknowledgment by apologizing, you demonstrate strength. But apologies aren't easy to make. What are some reasons why people don't want to apologize?

They don't like confrontation.

They think something was done to them first or that was worse.

The person to whom they're apologizing will rub it in their face.

It feels weak, like they are losing power or face.

Even under the best of circumstances, it's weird and uncomfortable.

A true apology . . .

- Expresses an understanding that what you did hurt someone.
- Demonstrates that understanding by saying "I'm sorry" in a genuine way.
- Is given without the expectation of a return apology.
- Addresses your actions alone.

An apology is *not* . . .

- Given with an excuse or justification ("I did it because . . .").
- Offered with an expectation of a return apology.
- Said with a condescending tone of voice.
- Given with another put-down at the end ("I'm sorry because you are . . .").
- Done to please someone with more social power than you.
- Done because you feel like you have to justify your feelings or what you want. ("Can you do your part of our group project? Sorry, but I just can't do it all.")
- Made to get something. ("I'm sorry. Now will you stop being mad at me?")

But sometimes it's hard for people really to believe apologies. For example, perhaps someone apologized, only to return to the same hurtful behavior. Are there any other reasons why you wouldn't trust someone's apology?

Giving and accepting apologies sincerely is powerful.

Often, when responding to an apology, the person will say, "It's okay," which can come across as if the problem didn't bother them in the first place. If you want your feelings to be taken seriously, say, "Thank you for the apology" instead of "It's okay." It's not a loss of power to admit that someone hurt you.

If you don't think the apology is genuine, say so, using SEAL to communicate your feelings. Here's a script you can consider if you get a fake apology:

> The way you just said "I'm sorry" doesn't seem like you mean it. If I'm wrong, tell me . . .

(Instructor note: If you have done the Act Like a Girl/Act Like a Boy Boxes, ask the students how the boxes can influence how people apologize based on gender expectations.)

ACTIVITY: Sincere and Insincere Apologies

Time: 15 minutes

Purpose: For better or worse, to use adults and often "leaders" to analyze sincere and insincere apologies

Ask students to do the following:

1. Look up "best and worst apologies" on your favorite internet search engine.
2. Pick one you think is a great example of a good genuine apology.
3. Choose one example of a fake apology.
4. Explain specifically what the person said, their tone, or their body language that made you decide it was a really good apology or a really bad apology.

Debrief/Takeaways

Apologies are a "window" into someone's character and what they perceive are their responsibilities to others.

Wrap It Up

Time: 5 minutes

- Anger is an understandable feeling to have. The goal is to process and communicate your feelings in a way that makes the situation better.
- SEAL is a strategy to help you do that. It won't make any problem you have magically go away, but it will give you more control over yourself and the conflict.
- Genuine apologies are powerful.

Carry It With You

- Earlier in the session, we came up with animals that represented our anger. For the next session, I'd like you to come up with an animal that represents the calm, powerful part of you that can quiet the angry animal part. Be ready to describe that animal at the next session.
- Is there anyone you should apologize to right now? If you answered yes to that question, challenge yourself to apologize before our next session.

The Power of Gossip

They Said *What?!*

This session shows students how normalized yet destructive gossip can be and how to develop strategies to stop it. By understanding this dynamic and its consequences, students are empowered to stop the damage they can do to themselves and others as well as to act in a more authentic and compassionate manner.

OBJECTIVES

- To define *gossip*
- To define *venting* so that students understand how to process their frustrating or confusing experiences with peers
- To understand why gossip "sticks" to some people more than others
- To demonstrate how gossip affects individual decision making and behavior
- To challenge the belief that someone's embarrassment is acceptable as entertainment for others

MATERIALS

- Whiteboard or flip chart
- Three signs, reading *Strongly Agree, Agree With Both,* and *Strongly Disagree*
- Paper and pencils
- Index cards
- Poster board and markers

Session Outline

What Are We Doing Today?

We are going to learn all the different ways gossip can affect our lives.

Review It

Time: 5 minutes

Last session we talked about SEAL. What animal did you come up with to describe the calm, wise part of you? Did you apologize to someone?

ACTIVITY: Does Gossip Matter?

THINK ABOUT IT

Time: 15 minutes

Purpose: To challenge the acceptance of gossip

Ask: Why do we gossip?

> It's fun.
> We're bored.
> We need something to talk about.

Let's look at two quotes from students. (*Instructor note: Choose two students to read the following quotes aloud*):

> It doesn't matter what people say. Sure, someone's reputation gets trashed for a few weeks, but then the gossip moves on to someone else. ("Ana")

> I hate how people keep getting into my business and judging me before they talk to me and find out the real story. ("Michael")

Debrief

- Is Ana right? Is gossip meaningless?
- Can it be "good" to be gossiped about? If so, how?
- Is gossip always true? Does it matter? For example, is it wrong to gossip if it's true but embarrassing or hurtful to the person you are gossiping about?
- Can anyone relate to what Michael said? How?
- If Michael feels this way at school, how does it affect his day? For example, while he's in class?

Takeaways

Gossip has the power to affect the way people feel about themselves and whether they feel comfortable (or not) around their peers.

ACTIVITY: Some Definitions

Time: 10 minutes

Purpose: To create a foundation for students to understand definitions they will apply throughout the sessions

Put the words stereotype, gossip, *and* venting *on the board. For each word, give a student an index card with the definition to read aloud.*

Ask: What is the definition of *stereotype?*

A stereotype is a widely held but fixed and oversimplified image or idea of a particular type of person or thing. There can be "negative" stereotypes and "positive" stereotypes, but both have some very important aspects in common: They don't allow the person to be seen as their own unique person, and they can make the person feel boxed or labeled in a way that makes them feel uncomfortable or disrespected.

Ask: What are some examples of a stereotype?

(Instructor note: If you do the Box exercises, you can refer to them as a source of stereotyping.)

Ask: What is the definition of *gossip?*

Gossiping occurs when you share information with the purpose of increasing your social status, bonding with someone, or trying to make someone look bad. The *Owning Up* definition starts the same way, but it's more complex:

> Gossip is like money. The more you have, the more power and influence you can have over your peers. Gossip also connects the people who are gossiping because there's an unspoken agreement among them that the person they're gossiping about "deserves" it, or it doesn't matter if they are hurt. The entertainment you're getting from gossiping is more important than the person feeling embarrassed, alone, or rejected. Even if one of the people gossiping doesn't actually agree with the gossip but says that they do, that agreement gives the gossip more power.

Ask: What part of that longer definition do you think is most important?

(Instructor note: While everyone, no matter their social status, can be gossiped about, gossip sticks to people in different ways. It sticks to people who are already socially vulnerable because of their race, socioeconomic status, ethnicity, sexual orientation, and/or gender expression. It "sticks" because our stereotypes about those identities reinforce the believability of the gossip. We see the target of the gossip less as a person in a particular circumstance and more as a reflection of the bias we already have.)

Ask: What is the definition of *venting?*

Venting occurs when you're mad at someone, and you talk to someone else about it to express your feelings and maybe talk about what you want to do about the problem.

Ask: Is there anything you want to add or take away from those definitions so we can make them our own?

Debrief

Is it easy for venting to cross into gossiping?

Takeaways

It can be hard to know the difference between the two unless you are aware of and honest about your motivations.

ACTIVITY: What's the Difference Between Venting and Gossiping?

Time: 15 minutes

Purpose: To clarify the difference between venting and gossiping

Everyone take out your index cards and write on one side "venting" and on the other side "gossiping/backstabbing." I'm going to read a statement aloud, you're going to close your eyes so you can't see what other people are doing, and I'll give you 10 seconds to decide if you think I've just described venting or gossiping. Once you decide, raise the index card with the word that matches your choice. After each one, I will ask people how they decided.

You tell a friend the following:

- You are really annoyed at another friend because they put themselves down all the time and you want to avoid them.
- You are really frustrated at another person in your group because they invite themselves to everything you do.
- A kid in school got in trouble for (a dress code violation, getting into a fight, etc.).
- One of your friends is about to dump someone.
- A fellow student wore something to school that looked really bad on them.

Debrief

- Did anything surprise you about what happened in the activity?
- What did you learn from the activity?
- How did you feel doing this exercise?

Takeaways

If you ask yourself, just for a moment, why you're sharing this information with the other person, you'll probably be able to know which one you're doing.

ACTIVITY: Knowing What to Do

Time: 20 minutes

Purpose: To develop self-awareness and responses to different gossiping situations

Say: It's easy to say what we should do, but it's usually way harder in real life to stop gossiping. And how gossip can come to us happens in different ways. For example, someone is talking about you, someone wants to tell you information about someone else, or you see gossip on social media.

Let's picture or write what we think happens in our brains when we find out that people are gossiping about us. Remember when we came up with animals that described how we feel when we are angry? Let's do the same to describe what happens when people are talking about us—when maybe we feel vulnerable or insecure. What animal represents our feelings in that moment?

Say: Now, let's come up with some things people say that aren't helpful when you find out people are saying bad things about you.

Examples:

> Don't let it bother you.
>
> Why do you even care?
>
> Let's get back at that person.

What are some things people can say that are helpful?

> If you really want to get back at them, don't try to get revenge because then they're controlling you.
>
> I'm really sorry. Is there anything I can do to make you feel better?

Debrief/Takeaways

You are always entitled to the feelings that you have. And you can't control your immediate emotional response. It's like someone popping a balloon behind you—you're going to be startled.

You don't have to become part of this power struggle. Understanding the motivation of gossip helps you consider what you say.

ACTIVITY: How to Make a Difference as a Bystander

Time: 15 minutes

Purpose: To take responsibility for stopping the cycle of gossip

Say: Close your eyes and raise your hand if you have ever gone along with the gossip/talking behind someone's back even though you really didn't agree or even though the gossip wasn't true.

When you are a bystander in a gossip situation, your goal is to help make the problem smaller, not bigger. Listening to the person and affirming their feelings makes the problem smaller. Wanting to help get revenge on the person who is gossiping makes the problem bigger. With that in mind, what would be a more helpful thing to say to support the person?

Here's a starting idea of what to say, but let's put in your own words:

I'm really sorry. Thanks for trusting me to tell me that. I'd be really upset if that happened to me.

ACTIVITY: What Happened on the Back of the Bus?

Time: 15 minutes

Purpose: To tie the lesson to scenarios the students can relate to

Read the following situation aloud, then discuss the questions.

There's a rumor circulating that a girl did something with a guy. She did do something with him, and she told her closest friends about what happened. Later, one of those girls tells a boy who's a friend of hers, and then he tells another friend. Within a day, everyone in the grade is talking about how this girl did something much more dramatic than what she actually did. The girl is really upset about the rumors. She tries to talk to the guy about it, but only on social media.

Debrief

- Is this situation realistic?
- Are there parts that are realistic? Why? Why not?

Takeaways

- People have the right to tell their close friends about important experiences.
- Those friends don't have the right to share that information.

ACTIVITY: Facing the Situation

Time: 20 minutes

Purpose: To help students develop responses for different dynamics around gossiping

What do you do if people are gossiping all around you?

Say: It's easy to feel trapped because it feels like whatever you say will be used against you.

What do you do if someone comes up to you and wants to tell you gossip?

Say: Take one moment and ask yourself, "Why does this person want me to know?" "Is this funny to me but really embarrassing to the person we're talking about?" "Why is this person telling me this?"

Does it matter if the gossip is true? Even if it is (and that can be really hard to know for sure), if you think there's a chance that the gossip is embarrassing or hurtful, then it's still wrong to talk about it. If you don't know if the gossip is true, not only are you contributing to hurting someone else, you are contributing to lies that will "stick" to them.

What if someone tells you someone else is spreading gossip about you?

Say: Take a deep breath, and then pay attention to what that person just told you. If they care about you and how you're feeling, it will show in the way they speak.

If they want to get you involved in the gossip or drama, they will ask you questions about what you are going to do about it.

If you have assessed that the person wants to drag you into the problem, what are some effective responses (online and in person)?

What if you tell a good friend a secret, they tell other people, and people are gossiping about you?

Say: You should be able to share with your close friends the things that are important to you. If you do and they tell other people, that can understandably feel like a really big violation of trust. So what do you do if you find out someone has violated your trust in this way?

If you confront the person who gossiped about you, what do they usually do?

> Make excuses.
>
> Blame someone else: "I only told that one person."
>
> Distract . . . They'll try to help the situation.
>
> Give a fake apology: "I didn't mean to hurt you."

What's the best response if they do any of the above?

Debrief

What are their tone of voice and body language telling you? Is it consistent or inconsistent with what they are saying?

Takeaways

It can be hurtful and confusing to have a close friend betray you. That doesn't mean you have to end the friendship, but you do need to ask yourself if you really can trust that person. This may be a time when you have to use SEAL to tell them how you're feeling about your friendship.

ACTIVITY: Student Pledge

Time: 15 minutes

Purpose: To have students choose one thing they want to change in their behavior and then try to hold themselves accountable

Give a student a large piece of poster board and a marker and ask him or her to record what you are writing on the board. Be clear with your students about where this poster is going to live, hang, etc. You can also do it as an online pledge as a Google doc or form.

Say: We are going to do a challenge—a kind of individual test. Who thinks your life would be easier if people did not do these kinds of things to each other? Do you think that's possible? Who would be willing to try?

Write: "We will . . ." at the top of the poster board.

Let's write down all the things you will try not to do to each other for a specific length of time, like "two hours after class" or "during lunch." We could even try for something huge, like "three days." If you're willing to try, you can write your name at the bottom of the pledge. If you don't think you can do it, then don't sign the pledge. We will appreciate your honesty.

Encourage students to be specific as to time and place, as in these examples.

We will not . . .

1. Whisper negative comments when we see someone walking down the hall.
2. Call anyone a bad, insulting name as we leave class today.
3. Gossip during lunch.

Debrief

Do you think it will be hard to stay true to the pledge?

Takeaways

Try your absolute best to stay true to the pledge. At the least try your best to remember what you pledged.

CHECK YOUR BAGGAGE

Since you are asking your students to be mindful about gossiping and to pledge to change their behavior, you should offer to do the same. Along with friends outside of the school, faculty, and family, add your name to the pledge and see if you can keep it.

Wrap It Up

Time: 5 minutes

- Gossip can control the things you say and what you do without your even realizing it.
- Being entertained or thinking something is funny shouldn't entail humiliating someone else.
- We think gossip is harmless until it's about us or someone we care about.
- If your friends can't support you for speaking out against gossip, then you need to review your standards of friendship. While it's true that you may lose a friendship for speaking out, your silence also comes at a price. You are in that friendship only if you go along with this messed-up system.
- If your friend speaks up for someone and you find yourself turning against the person, have the courage to look at your actions and hold yourself accountable.
- Your ticket out the door: Imagine that the feelings you've had during this session are colors. What colors have you felt during this session?

Carry It With You

Remember what you committed to stop on the pledge. Try your best to carry that pledge with you until our next session.

Reputations and Double Standards

Keep It? Lose It? Change It?

This session focuses on how gossip affects students' reputations and how those reputations have the ability to control students' actions. Students also learn about how double standards trap young people by controlling gender-based reputations, causing them to behave in ways that may not be true to themselves. Understanding how reputations and double standards are connected with gossip, stereotypes, and emotional resilience allows students to confidently challenge judgments made about others in a meaningful way.

OBJECTIVES

- To help students understand the link between gossip and reputations
- To understand how double standards work to influence individual behaviors and group dynamics
- To empower students with the skills to break these patterns and be more authentic and compassionate to themselves and others

MATERIALS

- Three signs with *Strongly Agree, Agree With Both, and Strongly Disagree*
- If you wish, index cards outlined with scenarios for the "Act It Out" role plays

Session Outline

What Are We Doing Today?

We are learning about the connection between gossiping and people getting labeled or stuck in reputations.

Review It

Time: 15 minutes

Say: Last session we wrote a pledge together that stated how long you were going to try to uphold a specific promise. While it would have been awesome if everyone who signed the pledge followed it the whole time, that's not really why we did it. *(Instructor note: Here's a great opportunity to show your students that you are holding yourself to the same standards you are asking of them. So if you made a pledge last session, you can discuss your experience here.)*

Debrief

- What was your pledge?
- How long were you able to keep your pledge?
- If you broke it, how did you feel?
- If you were able to keep it, how did you feel?
- Why do you think we made that pledge if there was a reasonable possibility that we would break it at some point?

Takeaways

We each made a specific pledge that we would take ownership of our behavior and be more mindful of our actions in the moment. It's usually really difficult to change our behavior overnight. It's a process. We are going to make mistakes, but we can own what we do.

ACTIVITY: How Do You Let Gossip Bounce Off You?

Time: 15 minutes

Purpose: To connect armor imagery with emotional resilience and gossip

Have you ever noticed that some people truly don't seem to care if others talk badly about them, some people pretend it doesn't bother them, and some people get really upset about it? Or maybe one kind of gossip doesn't matter to someone, but another kind really does? No matter where you fit on that spectrum, if you're in a situation where you're really upset or someone else is, we need to come up with some strategies to help the gossip bounce off you.

Let's go back to the image of armor we discussed in earlier sessions. Remember: You have the right to get upset when people gossip about you. You need some protection. I'm going to give you a piece of paper so you can draw your armor. Visualize the armor: What does it look like? What is it made of? What color is it? Are there words on it, and if so, what are they? This time let's draw and/or describe armor that can protect you from gossip. This way, if people are saying hurtful things about you in the future, you can close your eyes for just a second, take a deep breath, and visualize this armor protecting you.

Ask a few students to share their armor drawing with the rest of the class. Students can ask questions about the drawing or add to their own if someone gives them a good idea about what they want to include in their drawing. They can take the drawing with them and put it in their locker or backpack so they can take it out and consult it if they have a problem.

ACTIVITY: Three Corners Exercise

Time: 10 minutes

Purpose: To challenge students to think about the connections between gossip and reputations

After a certain amount of gossiping, the information "sticks" to the person and a reputation is formed. First, I'm going to read some statements aloud. When I do, I want each of you to think about the statement and then walk to the sign that best matches your opinion about it. Remember to be ready to share your thoughts!

1. Once you get a reputation, good or bad, you will always have it.
2. You should always back up a friend when he or she gets a bad reputation.
3. It is better to have a bad reputation than no reputation.
4. Usually, people deserve the reputations they have.

After you read each statement, give students a few minutes to move to a sign and discuss their position. Have at least one student at each location explain their decision to the larger group.

ACTIVITY: The Power of Reputations

Time: 20 minutes

Purpose: To define *reputation* and its influence on self-identity

THINK ABOUT IT

The dictionary definition of *reputation* is a widespread belief that someone or something has a particular habit or characteristic. The way *Owning Up* defines the word *reputation* is that it's a way to feel judged and trapped by other people's expectations and assumptions.

Break students into small groups (three to five students per group) and have each group answer the following questions.

Group 1

- Does the community that you live in have a reputation? How do you feel about that?
- What types of reputations can a girl have?
- What is the worst thing about having a good reputation?

Group 2

- What reputation does your school have? Do you think it is accurate? How do you feel about your school's reputation?
- What does a girl have to do to get a bad reputation?
- What does a boy have to do to get a bad reputation?

Group 3

- Is there a school that you have strong feelings about (either good or bad) based on its reputation? Is that fair?
- What does a girl have to do to get a good reputation?
- What is the worst thing about having a bad reputation?

Group 4

- What is the best thing about having a good reputation?
- What is the best thing about having a bad reputation?
- What does a boy have to do to get a good reputation?

Debrief

Each group reports back one question and the responses they want to share with the rest of the group.

Takeaways

Reputations are usually tied to many concepts we've already covered, including Act Like a Girl/ Act Like a Boy Boxes and stereotypes.

ACTIVITY: Double Standards

THINK ABOUT IT

Time: 5 minutes

Purpose: To define *double standard* and apply it to the situations the students just discussed

A double standard is a rule or principle that is unfairly applied in different ways to different people or groups.

Did you notice any double standards in people's answers in the small-group responses?

Now I want you to look for other double standards that may come up for you in the other topics for this session.

ACTIVITY: Fruit Cup Girl and Tough Guy

Time: 15 minutes

Purpose: To define *Fruit Cup Girl* and *Tough Guy* and how these gender roles influence behavior when people are attracted to each other

One of the more frustrating experiences in middle school can occur when a girl acts less intelligent and capable around boys. It's also frustrating when a boy acts more insensitive and tough in "public" than he really is. If you remember the definition of *culture*—"everything you just know but have never been sat down and taught"—think about how that applies here. No one tells a girl to scream when she sees a bug or pretend she doesn't understand what's going on around her, and no one tells a boy to make fun of a person when he's around someone he likes. Yet somehow boys and girls "know" how to do that. That's the influence of culture on people's behavior.

For the girl we named this phenomenon "Fruit Cup Girl" in honor of a sixth-grade student who pretended she couldn't open her fruit cup at lunch so she could ask the boy she liked to open it for her. What are the pros and cons of being Fruit Cup Girl (FCG)?

Pros of Being Fruit Cup Girl

- You get boys' attention.
- Your social status can go up when you get attention from boys.
- You are the center of attention.

Cons of Being Fruit Cup Girl

- You are liked for presenting yourself as less intelligent and capable than you really are.
- You may feel like this is the only way to get people's attention.
- Your behavior may convince people that they don't have to respect you.
- If it becomes a pattern, you can forget your true character and personality.

What Happens When You Observe Fruit Cup Girl?

- If you're a girl, you can feel embarrassed and angry because FCG is making all girls look bad.
- If you're a girl, you can feel jealous and confused because she's getting attention.

- If you're a boy, you can feel puzzled why girls act like that.
- If you're a boy, you can feel like all girls are less competent than you are.

For Tough Guy, a boy can change posture, vocabulary, or mannerisms around others. Tough Guy comes off as indifferent in his feelings toward girls, and he tends to treat them as objects to reinforce his social status.

Pros of Being Tough Guy

- You get girls' attention.
- Your social status goes up with other people because you are getting attention from girls.
- You look like you're in control and confident.

Cons of Being Tough Guy

- You are not being yourself.
- You pretend you're someone you're not.
- You pretend you don't care about things.
- If it becomes a pattern, you can forget your true character and personality.
- You bury your feelings until you don't have them anymore.

What Happens When You Observe Tough Guy?

- If you're a girl, you can be angry that Tough Guy doesn't listen to you.
- If you're a girl, you can be angry that other boys don't stand up to Tough Guy.
- If you're a guy, you can be wary of showing your own emotions.
- If you're a guy, you can feel frustrated that girls like Tough Guy more than they like you.
- If you're a guy and Tough Guy is your friend, you can feel self-conscious.

Debrief

Do you agree? Why or why not? How does it connect to the Act Like a Girl/Act Like a Boy Boxes or armor?

Takeaways

All of what we described doesn't have to reflect your experiences, but thinking about these dynamics can help you better understand people's behavior.

ACTIVITY: How Everything Connects

Time: 15 minutes

Purpose: To show what happens when gossip, reputations, double standards, and stereotypes combine

Last session we talked about a situation where people spread rumors about a girl and what she did with a boy, and the gossip firestorm that followed. Can someone remind us of what happened and what we discussed?

In that scenario, gossip, reputations, double standards, and stereotypes are invisibly directing people's thoughts and behavior. So, we are going to go back to that situation and discuss how gossip turns into a reputation. Remember, in the guidelines you can say "bad" words if they are related to the issues we are discussing and that may be relevant here. Even if they're uncomfortable to say in a classroom or write down (like I am going to ask you to do now), it's also possible that these are words you hear a lot after school, in the hallways, on the playground, during games, in your neighborhood, and online. *(Based on what you think is best for your students, tell them they are either going to keep their words private or share them.)*

Write it down: What are the most painful or worst reputations or labels a girl can get here?

What are the most painful or worst reputations or labels a boy can get here?

Debrief

Where do these words come from, and how can they have such power to hurt someone? *(If you've done the Box exercises, refer back to them here.)*

Takeaways

The word *slut* and all of its variations are used to portray women only as sexual objects who don't have the right to have an opinion or to be treated with dignity. Calling a girl, including your friends, these words may seem like not a big deal, but it is. It can seem uptight or making too much of it if you say something about it. But just because you see or hear something every day doesn't make it right. We also know that it can be confusing for guys when girls call each other sluts or present themselves in ways that conform to the slut reputation. But as we've learned in these sessions, people can do things without realizing why they're doing them.

(Instructor note: Older students may challenge the assumption that these words are bad because they have appropriated them and given them a positive meaning. If this occurs, have a discussion with two things in mind: First, under what conditions is it empowering to use these words? Second, how would you communicate that to others?)

ACTIVITY: Being Trapped in a Reputation

THINK ABOUT IT

Time: 10 minutes

Purpose: To acknowledge that a person can feel trapped in a positive or negative reputation

Debrief

What are some words that describe how a person could feel if they were trapped in a reputation? Is there a similarity between that feeling and people making comments about you or another person based on a stereotype?

Takeaways

No one likes feeling trapped by other people's judgments because they can limit what you do or say and convince you to act in ways that you feel may not be true to who you really are.

Wrap It Up

Time: 5 minutes

- No adults, including me, can control what you say. Only you can. But now that you know more about reputations, stereotypes, and double standards, you have the ability to decrease the power of these dynamics that hurt so many people.

- It may be unrealistic to hope that these sessions on gossip and reputations will completely stop people from saying mean things about each other. And, indeed, there will be people who may not take these sessions seriously. But ask yourself, why? What does a person have to lose by believing they can do something to stop the cycle of gossip and reputations?

- Your ticket out the door: How can you apply what we learned in class today to something in the world outside of school?

Carry It With You

Distribute "Handout for Interviewing an Adult" (Appendix F).

Say: Talk to a person in your family, or an adult you are close to or want to get to know better, about the experiences they had when they were your age. Record their answers to these questions on this page or on a separate sheet of paper.

The Power of Groups

Friendships, Strategic Alliances, or Both?

This session gives students the ability to identify common roles people may play in groups and how those roles may direct their interactions with others. While it is always a possibility that social dynamics occurring outside the classroom will affect participation in the classroom, the content of this session may make this issue particularly relevant. For example, a socially dominant person may silence others, or a student won't engage in the session because they're so alienated or intimidated by the group dynamics that they don't see the point in challenging them. The goal, at the least for the student, is to begin to understand the impact of these dynamics on themselves and others.

OBJECTIVES

- To identify typical social roles in the Act Like a Girl/Act Like a Boy Boxes and discuss behaviors and attitudes associated with groups

- To help students realize that they have control over what roles they choose to play in groups and encourage them to have more "keystone moments"—when they're able to unlock their understanding of their behavior and/or reactions to other people

- To give students the opportunity to practice SEAL with awareness of the workings of typical social roles

- To affirm the need to stand up for people who are being treated unethically, regardless of what group they belong to

MATERIALS

- Paper and pencils
- Copies of the "Act Like a Girl" and "Act Like a Boy" handouts (see Appendix G)
- Optional: Drawing paper and markers

Session Outline

What Are We Doing Today?

We are learning about the positives and negatives of friend groups.

Review It

Time: 5–10 minutes

Let's do a quick check-in about our last session. What do you think was the most important thing you learned? It could have been from videos, a comment someone made in class, or something you thought about.

Or (if you don't do the race sessions, or if you put the sessions in another order), split the class into groups of 6–8 and give each group a beach ball. On the ball are written questions. Each person in the group passes the ball to another person in the group. The catcher answers the question closest to his or her left thumb. See Appendix H for examples of beach ball questions.

ACTIVITY: Why Do We Have Groups?

THINK ABOUT IT

Time: 10 minutes

Purpose: To acknowledge the positive attributes of a group of friends while setting the stage for talking about a group's possible challenges

A group of friends can be one of the best parts of middle school. It can also be one of the most complicated and frustrating parts. People within a group can get mad at each other and too involved in one another's business, and most people will experience feeling excluded, picked on, or the odd one out. You can feel caught between two people fighting within your group and feel confused about where your loyalties should go. Or you could feel stuck in a particular position in your group. The purpose of this session is to bring up these situations and give you some new ways to think about them. Let's begin by writing a list of top-five positive and negatives about friend groups:

Positives

1. They're fun
2. People bring different things to the group
3. You get to hang out at different people's houses
4. It feels good to spend time with a group you feel close to
5. The group can support you when you have problems

Negatives

1. People in the group get into fights
2. You have to choose sides
3. You feel stuck in your group
4. It feels disloyal to hang out with other groups
5. A group can have a reputation you may not like

ACTIVITY: The Pros and Cons of Groups

Time: 20 minutes

Purpose: To give students the opportunity to safely share their true feelings and experiences about group dynamics

Say: I'm going to hand out a piece of paper and a pencil. On your sheet of paper, I want you to answer a couple of questions anonymously, so don't put your name on it. I'll collect your answers, and then I will read them aloud. If you don't want your answers read aloud, write "For Your Eyes Only" at the top of the page. Remember, it's okay to feel uncomfortable, but it's not okay to feel unsafe.

- Do you think there are groups at this school?
- How does the fact that these groups exist make you feel?
- How do you think these groups make other people feel?
- How do groups help or hurt your school/grade?

Debrief

- How did it feel to write those answers on the paper?
- How did it feel to give me the paper?
- How did it feel to hear what other people wrote?

Takeaways

Everyone's experiences with friendships are equally true. Even if your experience with friendships is different from what you heard, other people's experiences are just as important as yours. But it's difficult to know these different opinions because it can feel too uncomfortable or risky to admit what you really think—especially if it's different than what people in your friend group say.

(Instructor note: This activity could be for the whole class. If the exercise inspires the students to have a good conversation, then give them the time they need. An extension/alternative could also be to mix up the comments and pass them to small groups and let them discuss them. Or hang onto them, type them up, and mix them up the next time you meet for small groups to discuss.)

ACTIVITY: Act Like a Girl and Act Like a Boy Roles

THINK ABOUT IT

Time: 20 minutes

Purpose: To define roles people can play in groups

Putting labels on people's behavior can be tricky because describing the behavior can easily slide into describing a person overall. Ideally, a label should be something a person decides to pick up and connect to themselves—even if that label is negative—because it gives them self-knowledge and insight into what they do and why. But a label is something a person can decide to "take off" if it no longer fits. While the roles we will talk about were created by other middle school students, they may not match up perfectly with all your experiences, so we can come up with other terms you think better fit your situation.

Organize the students into small groups, and give each group a copy of the "Group Roles: Pros and Cons" handout (Appendix I).

Ask for a different volunteer to read each role aloud. Then have each student fill out the pros and cons worksheet. Once that is done, ask the following questions.

Debrief

- Do these roles apply at your school?
- At lunch, have you ever seen a guy or girl get up, and other people follow them?
- Does everyone fit in a role?
- Do you think a person's role ever changes? If so, what influences that change?
- What do you feel about these roles?
- Do you think these roles are helpful or hurtful in your school?
- People can get stuck in their role in a group. They can also play different roles in different environments. Can you give examples?

Takeaways

- Try to think of these roles as tendencies or moments.
- People in these groups can be really close friends. However, even though that's true, it's also true that negative power dynamics like the ones we're discussing can still exist in the same friendships.

ACTIVITY: Applying SEAL to Group Conflict

Time: 20 minutes

Purpose: To show students how to break down a conflict and think through solutions more effectively

Now that you know some of the typical roles people play in groups, let's try using SEAL to strategize a solution to common conflicts that occur in groups. Read the following situation aloud for the group and ask them if they can identify each character's role.

> Ilana, India, and Liz are close friends. Sometimes they hang out with Sara, a girl who really wants to be in their group. Sara overhears Ilana inviting India to her house and asks if she can come. Ilana tells Sara that her mom will only let her have one friend over. Sara later sees on her phone that the other girls were all hanging out at Ilana's house.

When there's a conflict in a group, it can be really confusing to figure out how the conflict occurred or how to think through the problem so you can figure out what to do. The chart below is a way to make the problem and the solution more clear.

	Sara	Ilana	India	Liz
Feelings	Nervous and rejected.	Irritated, impatient.	Annoyed at Sara and loyal to Ilana.	Wants to help Sara but is afraid to confront Ilana.
Motivations	Wants to be included.	Wants to do what she wants.	Wants Ilana to know that she is loyal.	Wants to be nice to Sara, yet maintain her friendship with Ilana and India.
Likely outcome	Tries harder, but pushes girls farther away.	Maintains control of the group.	Friendship with Ilana feels stronger, but it really isn't.	Doesn't say anything when she sees something wrong. Wonders if it could happen to her?
Consequences	Loses friends.	Friends are afraid to confront her.	Reinforces Ilana's right to be Queen Bee.	Learns to be silent in the face of cruelty.
Ideal outcome	Realizes these girls may not want to be her friends, but doesn't feel like she has to keep chasing them.	Learns that other people's feelings have to be balanced against her own.	Doesn't back up Ilana when she does something wrong. Realizes her role.	Confronts Ilana about her behavior and sticks up for Sara. Learns that she can disagree with her friends.

ACTIVITY: Role-Play a SEAL Strategy Around the Conflict

Time: 15 minutes

Purpose: To use SEAL to think through the conflict

Stop: Who is the conflict with, and what is it about? When and where will Sara talk to Ilana?

Explain: How is Sara feeling, and what does she want to happen?

Affirm and acknowledge: What rights do Ilana and Sara have in the situation? What is Sara's role in the conflict?

Lock: What does Sara want her relationship with Ilana to be?

Ask for volunteers to role-play the parts of Sara and Ilana. First enact the role play as the students think it would most likely happen. Then, as a class, have them come up with a possible strategy for Sara to speak to Ilana using SEAL.

Here's an example of a SEAL conversation:

Sara: Hey, Ilana, can I talk to you for a minute?

Ilana: Yeah, okay, sure.

Sara: You told me you could only have one person over, but I know Liz went to your house, too.

Ilana: (Pushback) No, she didn't. I mean, it was a last-minute thing because she was really upset about something with her parents, but I can't really tell you about it.

Sara: Why didn't you want to tell me the truth?

Ilana: (Pushback) I'm not lying! This is exactly the reason I didn't want to invite you. No offense, but you make such a big deal out of everything, and we needed to be there for Liz because she's having a really big problem, but I can't tell you about it.

Sara: Ilana, all I am asking is that you tell me the truth. If you want me to give you some space, I can.

Debrief/Takeaways

- It's really common for people to join a new group and then leave an old friend behind. When that happens it can be really hurtful to the person left behind.
- Even if you were really close friends in the past, you can't force someone to be your friend now.
- Even if you did succeed in forcing them to be your friend again, what do you think would most likely happen?
- What happens if you give a friend space?

ACTIVITY: Choosing Sides

Read the following situation aloud for the group and ask them if they can identify each character's role.

Wyatt, Aiden, Anthony, and Kevin are all close friends. After lunch they always play basketball with some other kids. Wyatt, as he often does, starts teasing Kevin about how bad he is, his hair, and how short he is. As always, Aiden joins in. They start playing, and other people start laughing and making fun of Kevin too. Kevin plays worse and worse. Anthony sees what's happening, and he doesn't like it.

	Anthony	**Wyatt**	**Kevin**	**Aiden**
Feelings	Nervous, conflicted whether it's really worth saying anything.	Powerful.	Rejected.	Powerful.
Motivations	Doesn't like people being humiliated, but doesn't want to risk friendships by saying anything.	Wants to demonstrate power.	Wants to be included and respected.	Wants to demonstrate loyalty to Wyatt.
Likely outcome	Doesn't say anything. Wonders if it could happen to him.	Maintains control.	Could try harder to be in the group, or give up.	Friendship with Wyatt feels stronger but isn't.
Consequences	Stuck and silenced.	Reinforces power. Learns that humiliating people is funny.	Becomes isolated.	Reinforces Wyatt's right to be the Mastermind.
Ideal outcome	Uses SEAL to articulate his feelings. Friendships with Wyatt and Aiden are strengthened.	Learns confidence doesn't come from putting others down.	Feels supported and included.	Learns confidence doesn't come from putting others down. Learns he doesn't always have to support his friends' decisions when they are acting unethically.

Imagine you are Anthony and you want to do something to address the problem.

Stop: Who is the conflict with, and what is it about? Should you say something to the rest of the guys while the conflict is occurring or wait? *(Explain your reasoning for either choice.)* Who do you need to approach to stop the situation from happening again?

Explain: How are you feeling, and what do you want to happen?

Affirm and acknowledge: What rights does Kevin have in the situation? What is Aiden's role in the conflict? Wyatt's role? Your role? Should you say anything to Kevin?

Lock: What do you want your friendship with Aiden or Wyatt to look like?

Ask for volunteers to role-play the two characters. Set the scene by saying the two are walking away from the playground, with other students ahead of them. First enact the role play as it would usually happen, and then use SEAL to come up with another approach to the conversation.

Sample SEAL conversation:

You: Hey, Wyatt, wait up!

Wyatt: Yeah?

You: Doing that thing to Kevin when we were picking teams was rough.

Wyatt: He knows he sucks! Anyway, it's not like he said anything.

You: But that was just rubbing it in. And he didn't say anything because you keep saying you're just joking.

Wyatt: Whatever.

You: Wyatt, it would have been way easier not to say anything, but we're friends, so I am. Just lay off of him, okay?

Takeaways

- This exercise is showing how SEAL can help create a bystander strategy. There are always going to be different ways to support someone who is maliciously teased and humiliated by someone else. SEAL helps you think your strategy through.

- It is a lot easier to say nothing to friends when they do something you don't think is right. But being a friend is about having these conversations.

- These conversations don't take a long time. You can have a good SEAL in a few minutes.

ACTIVITY: Should You Ever Break Up With Your Group?

THINK ABOUT IT

Time: 10 minutes

Purpose: To connect individual friendship rights with one's rights within a friend group

Just as you created friendship rights and deal-breakers for individual friendships, you should have the same rights and deal-breakers in your group. There could many reasons, or just one. Maybe you feel like your group wants you to be only one way? For example, if you changed your personality, would they accept that change?

What is the worst thing that could happen if you broke up with your group?

What is the worst thing that could happen if you stayed in the group?

Is there another group you identify with more?

> **Fake loyalty:** Supporting or agreeing with someone even if they are doing something you don't agree with or know is wrong
>
> **True loyalty:** Supporting someone when it's hard, unpopular, and may cost you in some way

What is your definition of *loyalty?*

Wrap It Up

Time: 5 minutes

- It can be really uncomfortable to think about a role you may play in a group, or you may deny that it applies to you and your friends. If you are feeling that way, sit with the feeling and later ask yourself why you had that response in the session.

- Often, how we respond as a bystander and our feeling of obligation to step in has more to do with how we feel about the people involved than the action that is taking place. As a bystander, try to separate your feelings and relationships with the people from your opinion about how people are treating each other.

- You have the right to hang out with people you want, but you don't have the right to be mean when you do it.

Carry It With You

- Be an ethnographer (a person who studies people). Apply what you have learned in this session by observing where and how people hang out in public places like the mall, bleachers during a game, on the school bus, and so on. Who looks like they have power? Who doesn't? How can you tell? Bring your observations to the next session to share.

- Before our next session, ask yourself the following question: If you are part of a group, what role (or roles) do you think you play? Are you happy with your role? Why or why not? If you're not happy with your role, what is one thing you can do to break out of your label?

Creating Your Style

Brand Names and Price Tags

SESSION 8

Creating and "choosing" a personal style is incredibly important to young people. It's also deeply personal. This session helps students learn how the media may be influencing their style choices. It teaches media literacy by focusing on how students are convinced to spend money on their image (a pair of shoes, a coat, the right cell phone) and why that can come at the cost of their personal authenticity. When teaching this session, it is important to avoid appearing to criticize the students for buying into these images. Be clear that everyone is influenced in this way and emphasize that the goal of the session is to make them aware of this influence so they can be more in control of developing their personal style in a way that is truly reflective of who they are.

OBJECTIVES

- To help students understand the connection between buying into the culture and choosing their music and clothes as a part of their self-identity and their choice of friendship group
- To encourage them to consider the importance of valuing people for who they are instead of what they have
- To encourage students to choose a more personally authentic style for themselves
- To connect to the individual armor that the students discussed in the first session
- To validate the right for students to experiment with their image as a process of adolescent development

MATERIALS

- Board or flip chart
- Scissors, magazines, 8.5″ by 11″ cardboard paper, glue, or tape
- Index cards

CHECK YOUR BAGGAGE

- When was the last time you bought something because you wanted it to help your image?
- When you were an adolescent, what did you buy or wear to enhance your image and/or popularity?

Session Outline

What Are We Doing Today?

Today, we are examining the development of our individual personal style and then deciding if it feels comfortable and/or true to our self-identity.

Review It

Time: 10 minutes

Write SEAL on the board, and as the students come into the room ask them to write down their own words for the "S" "E" "A" "L".

Say: The Carry It With You from the last session was about groups. So I'm going to give you a piece of paper as I did last time and ask you to answer one of the questions from the Carry It With You. Is there any role you play that you want to think about changing? Why?

Collect the papers and then read the responses aloud as you did in the previous session.

Debrief

Are there any patterns we heard?

Takeaways

Give you and the people around you the freedom to break out of roles you don't like.

ACTIVITY: You or Not You?

THINK ABOUT IT

Time: 15 minutes

Purpose: To get students to think about authentic style—theirs or someone else's

Say: Now we are going to examine another aspect of ourselves—our personal style. Break into small groups and answer at least two of the following questions among the people in the group.

- What purchase have you made or someone made for you that you value the most? Why is it so important to you?
- Think of the last purchase you made that disappointed you. How did you think your life would be better if you got it? Is your life better for having this thing?
- Think of a celebrity whose image and style you like. What do you like and why?
- Think of a celebrity whose image and style you don't like. What don't you like and why?
- How would your friends react if you changed your image?
- If you had a good friend who changed his or her image in a way you really didn't like, could you still maintain the friendship? Why or why not?

Debrief

How did your group answer the questions? Was there total agreement or a difference of opinion?

Takeaways

We can be influenced to buy certain things or look a certain way because it seems cool, even though that might not be true to who we are or what we want.

ACTIVITY: The Collage of Wants

Time: 20 minutes

Purpose: To identify how students may be influenced by advertising in developing what they perceive to be their personal style

Give out magazines (make sure they're a variety of magazines), scissors, glue, and cardboard paper (if you don't have cardboard paper, just have the students cut out the images they choose). Have the students select pictures of things they want to buy, and create an individual collage. Use the collages to generate a discussion about students' self-image and how they value others.

Ask:

- What pictures did you choose for your collage?
- What do your choices say about you?
- How do you think your life will change if you get the things you selected?

Ask the following questions and discuss how self-presentation and style are a way in which girls and guys create the image they wish to project.

- What is your style?
- How do you display your style?

- What do you want your style to say about you?
- Do your friends have a different style than yours? If your friends have the same style as you, why do you think that is?
- Where else do you feel pressure about style or image? *(Perhaps, for middle schoolers, the other pressure they feel is from their families; this can be a great source of conflict/angst).*

Say: Here's a quote from a seventh grader:

> Everyone in my school has a particular kind of leggings and if you don't have that brand you can be standing right next to people but feel left out and disconnected. But it feels weird to have this feeling because there's really no reason to have this feeling. It's your own feeling of not fitting in but it still really bothers me. I know it's superficial but I still feel that way. ("Izzy")

Say: I can relate to this feeling—I think all people can. When I was your age, I wanted X because I thought my life would be better in Y ways. Even recently, I had a similar experience. I saw X and really wanted it. But I had to stop and ask myself why I wanted it so badly.

Debrief

- Can you relate to how Izzy feels?
- Who told Izzy and the other girls in her group that those leggings were the ones they had to have?
- Why did they want Izzy and her friends to believe that?
- How did they convince Izzy and her friends?

Takeaways

- We are all influenced by what we see in the media.
- Seeing those messages can affect how we feel about ourselves in negative ways.
- Being aware when this is happening takes away some of the power the media hold over us.

ACTIVITY: Transform Your Image

Time: 15 minutes

Purpose: To challenge students to create a self-style and image that more closely reflects their true self

It's a common experience to feel disconnected from your friends if you don't have the same things, and you get messages from the media trying to make you focus on your outside image. So let's refocus on your core self. Everyone needs a motto or mantra to help them concentrate on how they want to live their lives.

Share a few examples:

> "Do what you're most afraid of."
>
> "Dignity is not negotiable."
>
> "I can be me without fear."
>
> "Just because you can doesn't mean you should."

Give students a few minutes to think, then have them say their mottos or mantras aloud. Write them on a sheet of poster board for everyone to see. If students have trouble thinking of a motto or mantra, you can suggest that they go to the library or the internet after the session and try to find inspiration there. They can share what they find at the next session. The students should try to find something that at the present moment, closely reflects their personality and feelings.

Debrief

How do you think a motto like this can help you? When do you think it would help you the most?

Takeaways

Mottos or mantras are yours. No one can take them away from you.

ACTIVITY: Why Do Parents Get So Uptight About What Kids Wear?

THINK ABOUT IT

Time: 15 minutes

Purpose: To present students with their parents' point of view about their style and image

Say: Has anyone had a parent or another adult disapprove of something you've worn? Even if you disagree with them, let's break into small groups and take a few minutes to see if we can come up with rational reasons why parents have these opinions. Then, come up with specific things you'd advise parents to say to effectively communicate with their children. (*If time permits, you could role-play one or more because young people usually like to imitate adults.*)

1. Your 12-year-old daughter starts wearing very revealing clothes. Do you say anything to her? What do you say?
2. Your 15-year-old son starts dressing, walking, and acting way tougher than he is. Do you say anything to him? What do you say?
3. You have a 13-year-old son who plays basketball and also loves theater. His friends on the team are teasing him about liking theater, and now he wants to give up being in the spring play. What advice would you give him?

4. Your daughter is begging you to buy her a pair of really expensive jeans. You know she wants them because all the girls in her group have them. Do you get them for her? What if you really can't afford them, so the only way you can pay for them is on credit?

Debrief

What were the most important insights your group discussed? What advice did you come up with?

Takeaways

Sometimes parents can have good reasons why they are concerned about what you want to buy.

Wrap It Up

Time: 5 minutes

- Your overall style says a lot about you, so it's important to know why you are making those choices. You want your style to be authentic—an extension of who you are on the inside.
- You can change it up—try new ways of looking and dressing.
- If you don't understand how the media are trying to convince you that you need certain things in order to be valued, the media control you. We want you to be in control of yourself.

Carry It With You

When you watch your favorite TV shows, videos, or games, pay close attention to see what advertisers are trying to convince you to buy. See if you can count them throughout the show. See if you can find any product placements during the show itself. For example, when a character is looking at a computer, can you see what kind of computer it is? Can you see what kind of drink the character is drinking? Once you start seeing one product placement, you'll probably start seeing them all over.

Managing Technology

Posts, Profiles, and Platforms

SESSION
9

We are all creating cultural norms around technology and social media. Young people reach out to others for support, to express their creativity, and to develop professional connections never even imagined before. Previously isolated, marginalized young people find and build communities online. On the other hand, young people's preoccupation with curating the ideal online image to gain and maintain a sense of belonging, approval, and popularity on social media drives their insecurity and anxiety. So what's the best way to reach them about managing technology in their lives?

We believe we will lose young people immediately if we teach technology from a fear-based approach as in, "If you send one embarrassing picture of yourself you will never get into college or get a job." Instead, a more effective strategy recognizes that the social media young people create and participate in reflect how they absorb and react to larger cultural messages. Many young people use social media responsibly. It is important to acknowledge that young people are creating private and public identities online that are tied to their identity development. In fact, sometimes those who struggle socially in person can communicate better online.

OBJECTIVES

- To connect social norms in real life to life online
- To self-reflect on the development of self-identity and how one chooses to communicate that identity in social media
- To affirm how important young people's online social communication is to their friendships
- To show potential consequences when personal identity is constantly tied to meeting other people's perceived expectations

MATERIALS

- Whiteboard
- Markers for at least five students to use at once

Session Outline

What Are We Doing Today?

We are learning about managing our information and image online.

Review It

Time: 5–10 minutes

Write Subliminal *with the definition under the word, and* Find Any Product Placements? *and* How Many? *on the whiteboard. As students come in, have them write their observations from last session's Carry It With You.*

Ask:

- What was the most obvious product placement you saw?
- What was the least obvious (best hidden) product placement you saw?
- Is there a connection between the product placements you saw and their intended audience?

ACTIVITY: What's Our Experience?

Time: 10 minutes

Purpose: To share our experiences with social media with other people in the group

We are going to think about how people use social media and how you want to express yourself online. We aren't talking about these issues with the assumption that any of them are terrible or that you that are addicted to social media. But it is a significant part of your life, so that's why we think it's important to discuss. First, we are going to check in about our experiences. I'll ask a question that starts with, "Have you . . ." and if you have had the experience, step into the circle and then step outside.

- Obsessed over your personal score on a social media platform?
- Had someone use your password without your permission?
- Been in school when someone showed you a post about you that made you feel bad?
- Had someone sign you up for a website without your permission?
- Been blamed for something you didn't do on social media?
- Had parents spy on what you're posting online?
- Had someone post a mean comment about a picture you posted?
- Been in school when you have seen a post about someone else that made you feel nervous or bad for the person?

- Played a game online and heard/read someone say mean things about people based on their race, sexual orientation, or other identifying features?

- Obsessed on how many likes you've gotten about something you posted?

- Had someone send an embarrassing photograph of you without your permission?

- Not told an adult (like a parent) about something bad that happened to you online because you were worried they'd take away your technology (like your phone) if you told them?

Debrief

What was interesting to you about how people answered? What was a hard question to admit it to, and why?

Takeaways

No matter who we are, most of us have had experiences on social media that are stressful or confusing.

ACTIVITY: Can You Relate?

Time: 20 minutes

Purpose: To examine how wanting social affirmation on social media can affect students' thinking and behavior

We're going to split into small groups, and I am going to give each group a quote to read and discuss. The quotes are from teens who are sharing one aspect of what they think about social media in their lives. You will have 10 minutes to discuss the quote I give you. Then we will come back together as a big group. One person from each group will read the quote aloud, as well as three insights the group decided were most important for everyone else in the class to discuss.

> **Group 1:** I've had my Instagram account for a couple years. On average, I get a little over 100 likes. If I post something and it gets fewer than 100 likes, I honestly consider deleting the photo. I have friends who've told me that they will delete any photo that gets fewer than a certain number of likes.

> **Group 2:** Kids are now not only judged harshly by others about how they look/act in person, but also they now have a separate internet life they're expected to post about and look and act good in. Now kids gossip about "Wow, did you hear what they said?" along with "Their comment to that post was so stupid and cliché." It's leading a double life, except you act the same and different in both of them at the right times. So many kids feel this anxiety about being judged by other kids based on how many notifications they have when they open up their phones or how many followers they have.

Group 3: The reason why kids are constantly on their phones isn't because they're addicted to the technology itself, but they're addicted to the need to check to see if their friend texted them back, or if that hot guy or girl liked their photo. As much as we may deny that we care about these things, we do.

Group 4: Something people may not know about me is that I have at least seven analytical apps that tell me about my followers on Instagram. I can see who looks at my profile and who likes my posts the most. Why do I do it? I want to know more about people and what they thought about me. It's interesting for me to have data on who shows interest in me. I don't know how much that contributes to what I think about myself.

Group 5: I want to share my life with people, but in an edited way. There's also a part of me that wants to be liked, so having the number comforts me. I like knowing there is a group of people who knows what's going on with me.

Debrief

- Is there a specific idea or insight your group discussed that stands out for you?
- Is there a specific idea or insight someone else shared that stands out for you?
- What pattern or patterns to the ideas or insights of the groups did you notice?
- Could people in your group relate to what the quote described?

Takeaways

If you're posting on social media where people can like what you post, it's easy to develop a pattern of behavior in which you're trying to please an imaginary audience. That being the case, how much of the "real" you are you showing versus the "ideal" you? And where are you getting the ideas of who is the "ideal" you? These questions will come up a lot in this session and the next one.

ACTIVITY: Pleasing the Imaginary Audience

THINK ABOUT IT

Time: 10–15 minutes

Purpose: To understand the connection between the pictures the students take and what they are trying to communicate to others

Gallery walk: Let's brainstorm all the possible reasons why people take selfies. Each student is given five sticky notes on which they have to write something at each question "station."

- What are the common poses you see people take?
- Where do they take them?
- What are they trying to communicate in the way they pose?
- Why do you think people choose to have a signature pose or look?
- What are the positives and negatives about taking selfies?

Debrief/Takeaways

- What images and words do girls post to communicate their personal images?

- What images and words do boys post to communicate their personal images? Are there similarities and differences?

- How are your social media posts a reflection or a resistance to the box you most closely associate yourself with?

- When you post something on social media, how much are you thinking about what you think other people expect to see about you?

ACTIVITY: Creeping on Yourself

Time: 15 minutes

Purpose: To have students self-reflect on how they might be trying to impress others

Say: Take out your phones and look back at 5–10 posts you shared six months ago or over the summer.

Debrief

We've been talking about the imaginary audience in your life right now. Now let's imagine your future audience. Who will those people be?

Ask students to write the answers down on the whiteboard. Note future girlfriends/boyfriends, colleges, employers.

If your audience looked at what you posted six months ago, what do you think they would believe about you? If they looked at what you posted in the last month, what assumptions or stories would they believe about you?

Takeaways

The images and words people choose in social media don't come out of nowhere. They choose them for a specific reason or reasons. Those reasons are a combination of the messages that come from their life experiences.

Wrap It Up

Time: 5–10 minutes

Finish the session with this stem exercise:

- Social media can make you . . . (have a constant need for affirmation from other people—sometimes people you don't even know)

- Social media can give other people . . . (a lot of power over how you feel about yourself)

- Social media can give you a lot of power . . . (when you judge people; as much as you may get upset when someone says something negative about you, it's easy to minimize the impact of what you do or say on social media)

- The positives of social media are . . .

- The negatives of social media are . . .

Carry It With You

If you aren't already doing this, try this for at least three days. Before bed, charge your phone outside your bedroom and don't look at it until 15 minutes before you leave for school the next morning. If you're really feeling ambitious, try not looking at your phone until lunch or after school! But whenever you do look at your phone, pay attention to your emotions as you look at the information. Are you happy? Sad? Anxious? Relieved to be catching up? Observe your posture as you look at your phone. Good luck!

The Mirror

Why Do I Try to Look Like This?

This session gives students the opportunity to learn and discuss gender appearance norms. But this session is not only about girls. While the pressure girls feel to "fit" certain gender expectations is well established, the same is not true for boys. Boys are pressured to conform to hypermasculinized standards of appearance in much the same way that girls are pressured to conform to hyperfeminized standards. However, girls not only possess a common language to discuss their experiences, but parents and educators are usually aware of these issues as well. In contrast, boys often feel like they don't have a language for discussion, let alone permission to talk about their feelings. This session offers students the opportunity to become aware of important issues that every student faces regardless of how they express their gender. This experience gives them a language to define the problem and permission to ask for support.

OBJECTIVES

- To make the connection between culturally defined standards of gender appearance and students' self-image
- To establish the connection between the culture's standards of gender and unhealthy body image
- To equally affirm girls' and boys' experiences with gender expectations

MATERIALS

- Whiteboard or flip chart
- Pictures from magazines such as *People* (and *People en Español*), *Seventeen*, *Vogue*, *Ebony*, and *Vibe*. The "Before and After" advertisements typically placed at the back of women's and men's fitness magazines are especially effective examples of cultural idealized male body types.
- Pictures, models, or media necessary to conduct the Toys Over Time activity
- Copies of the "Eating Disorders" handout (see Appendix J)
- Index cards
- Colored stickers or markers
- Sticky notes
- Paper and pencils

Session Outline

What Are We Doing Today?

We are learning about what makes us judge each other and ourselves based on certain physical expectations.

Review It

Time: 10 minutes

The following activity is based on the Carry It With You from the last session, so it is based on the material you covered in the last session as well.

1. *Give each student an index card as they enter the room.*

2. *On the front board, whiteboard, etc., write the following instructions:*

   a. On your index card, write a 140-character "tweet" with an original hashtag to describe what it was like to put your phone outside your bedroom for Session 9's Carry It With You assignment.

   b. When done, share your "tweet" with a partner and then put it up on the class wall.

3. *When all students have put up their "tweets," give each student five colored stickers or markers (to retweet or favorite some index card "tweets") and five sticky notes (to reply to some index card "tweets").*

4. *Discuss with students what they learned by checking out one another's index card tweets.*

5. *Optional (if time): Have students work together to arrange/classify the index card "tweets" by trends.*

ACTIVITY: Toys Over Time

Time: 20 minutes

Purpose: To link media literacy with students' perceptions of gender

Ask students to do the following:

- Find images online of male action figures and "most popular toys for boys" from the 1960s to the present.

- Find images online of female action figures and "most popular toys for girls" from the 1960s to the present.

Debrief

- What differences do you notice?
- What types of toys were you given the most when you were a child?
- Did you like them, or did people assume you would like them?

Now let's look specifically at toys marketed to children today.

Have the students form small groups, as they will be looking through catalogs (paper or online) for toys marketed to young children. After groups are formed:

1. *Give each group one or more toy catalogs.*
2. *Ask the students to go through their catalogs and pick out two or three toys.*
3. *Have them explain who they think is the toy company's targeted customer, and why. How do they know that? (For example, the toys' color, decorations, or design.)*
4. *Reassemble the larger group and discuss.*

Ask: What do the toys teach younger children about the "right" way to act like a boy or girl? Do the toys reflect any other stereotypes in our culture? If so, what are they?

Takeaways

Toys can influence how children understand how they're "allowed" to play. It's another example of how children are taught invisible rules about what's acceptable for them to do or even feel. So think about the armor you have now that we drew and discussed. There may be a connection between what you learned through the toys you played with and how your armor developed into what it is today.

ACTIVITY: Where Does the Ideal Look Come From?

THINK ABOUT IT

Time: 15 minutes

Purpose: To have students connect cultural societal gender expectations with their own gender expectations

Obviously, people aren't born feeling worthless, but there can be several reasons why they can come to feel this way *(note that not all reasons are listed below).*

For example:

1. Being over a goal weight
2. Having the wrong hair (color, texture, or style)
3. Having not enough muscles
4. Being too "bulky"
5. Having the wrong-size nose
6. Being too small or too big

Engage students in discussion:

- Describe the characteristics society (or our culture) says girls need to have to be considered physically attractive.
- Describe the characteristics society (or our culture) says boys need to have to be considered physically attractive.

Write their responses in two columns in the center of the board or flip-chart paper. Ask students to do the following:

- Describe the characteristics society doesn't want girls to look like or define as attractive.
- Describe the characteristics society doesn't want boys to look like or define as attractive.

Write these responses around the words you first wrote. Finally, draw a box around the first set of words, as the sample diagram shows.

Girls: Is There a Right Way to Look?

Bad skin	Straight/thick head of hair	
	No body hair	
Overweight	Good teeth/smile	Bad teeth
	Clear skin	
Too skinny on the outside	Thin, but has the right curves	Bad grooming (hair and nails not done)
	In shape, but not too bulky	
Hairy	Light colored (blue/green) eyes or "Western" eyes	Big feet
Bad hair	Good grooming (nails done, good hair)	

Boys: Is There a Right Way to Look?

Bad skin	Straight/thick head of hair	Hairy
Short	Right amount of body hair in the right places	Bad hair
Overweight	Good teeth/smile	Bad teeth
Too skinny	Clear skin	Bad grooming
	Tall	
	Good grooming	

It's really hard to do this exercise and not think about where you fit or don't fit in the box. It's also really hard to do this exercise and not think about where other people fit. It *is* easy to do this exercise and compare yourself to others. But that's not what this exercise is about. Instead, it's about how these rules of appearance can influence us—both how we feel about our own bodies and those of other people.

- Where do these messages come from? Who is saying them to you?
- How much do you think these boxes affect the adults in your school?
- How much do you think these boxes affect people your age?

Note: In the original body style in 1964, if GI Joe were a man in real life, he would measure 5 feet 8 inches tall. He would have a 32-inch waist, 44-inch chest, and 12-inch bicep. This is similar to the average fit male.

By 1974, GI Joe was reconfigured so that his bicep was 15 inches.

In 1991, the waist and chest shrank slightly, to 29 and 43 inches, respectively, but the biceps grew to 16.4 inches (as big as those of most competitive bodybuilders). In 1998, GI Joe Extreme was released, boasting a "real-life" 36.5-inch waist, 55-inch chest, and nearly 27-inch biceps—larger than any bodybuilder in history.

ACTIVITY: Using SEAL

Time: 20 minutes

Purpose: To expand the use of SEAL to include communicating in the following uncomfortable situations

Act It Out: Fishing for Compliments

You have a friend, Elise, who is really getting on your nerves because she is always complaining about how fat and ugly she is. You tell her she's not fat, but nothing you say makes her feel any better. It's like she's always fishing for compliments. It's crossed your mind to agree with her the next time she puts herself down. Part of you feels bad for her, but another part of you is getting really annoyed. Worse, she's beginning to make you question your own weight and appearance.

Debrief

Let's try to understand Elise's motivations before you think about what you want to say to her. Why does she say she's fat when she's not? *(If students say, "She's insecure," dig deeper to find out what is behind her insecurity.)*

Why does her behavior bother you so much? *(If they say, "Because it's annoying," challenge them to be more specific.)* Could this be a venting/talking behind someone's back moment?

Sample Dialogue

You: Elise, I need to talk to you.

Elise: Are you mad at me or something?

You: No, I'm not mad at you, but I need to talk to you about the things you say about yourself.

Elise: Okay . . .

You: When you say you're fat or put yourself down about how you look, I tell you you're not, but it doesn't make a difference. I want you to feel good about yourself, but I don't want to feel like I have to do this all the time.

Elise: I'm sorry. I'm sorry. I know it's so stupid.

You: Don't apologize for feeling bad. But we need to do something. Is there any way we could think about someone else you could talk to who really knows about this stuff?

Act It Out: Shirts Versus Skins

Brian is in (your students' grade) and he loves playing basketball. During practice, the coach separates the teams by "shirts" and "skins." Brian knows that Ben hates taking his shirt off because the other boys tease him about his chest.

Ask: What are options Brian has in this situation?

- Talk to the coach? If so, what should he say?
- Talk to the other guys about it? Which guy, and why? What would he say to him?
- Talk to Ben about it?
- Say something to support Ben if one of the other guys teases him about it? If so, what should Brian say?

Takeaways

Every one of us is affected by the messages we get about how we should and shouldn't look.

ACTIVITY: Throw Away the Negatives

Time: 10 minutes

Purpose: To have students process the feelings they experienced during the session and feel empowered to reframe their self-image

1. *Have the students privately write down anything they don't like about their bodies or that people have told them they need to change about their bodies.*

2. *Then help them discard their "negatives" in the most creative way possible (e.g., crumple them up, tear them into tiny pieces). Have students get into a circle and do this one by one.*

3. *After the negatives have been discarded or destroyed, ask, "What did it feel like to throw away the negatives?"*

Debrief/Takeaways

"Throwing away" the negatives that preoccupy you and bring you down gives them less power to make you feel bad. You aren't so controlled by them. Remember this when you feel those negatives weighing you down.

Wrap It Up

Time: 5 minutes

- Children are influenced about gender expectations at very early ages.
- Both boys and girls are under pressure to conform to certain gender looks.
- No one is born feeling insecure about how they look.

Carry It With You

- Give a compliment to two adults you know—one woman and one man—and pay attention to their response. Do they say, "Thank you," or do they put themselves down? What does their response say to you about what we discussed during this session?

- If you have toys or games in your house, think about how they "match" or "don't match" with what we discussed in the session. You can also look up new toy companies that are making less gender-specific toys and see what you think about them (http://www.iamelemental.com). Be ready to discuss them at our next session.

Race and Bias

What Do We Really See?

SESSION
11

The last session focused on gender norms and expectations. This session builds on how cultural norms combine with racial and ethnic stereotypes to influence young people's perceptions and behavior. This session isn't only for the benefit of students of color. It will increase the majority races' and ethnicities' awareness, consideration, and empathy for their minority race/ethnic peers.

Because these issues are so rarely discussed in an open forum, students may approach the session with anxiety, defensiveness, confusion, or ignorance. These reactions are natural and understandable. Your responsibility here, as in all the sessions, is to allow for the discomfort while maintaining the dignity of everyone in the room. If the dynamics in the session become too uncomfortable, go back to the anonymous writing exercise outlined in the book's Introduction. Or you can do a metaphor/analogy check in by asking, "Okay, everyone, if this session were a song, animal, or food, what would it be?" Or you could ask the students to describe their feelings by coming up with a haiku, cinquain, or other form of poetry.

Frame your introduction to the session by assuring your students that while they're inheriting a legacy of people struggling with racism and talking about racism, they didn't create this system. But they are living in it. You should also admit that it's unusual for adults to talk to students about these issues in this way, but you believe these students are mature and smart enough to do it. If nothing happens but your students discuss these issues, sit with their discomfort, and then process these feelings respectfully with their peers, the session will have been a success.

OBJECTIVES

- To create an environment where students can think about how media messages impact their beliefs about race and ethnicity
- To teach students a process of self-reflection on how racial stereotypes impact their thinking
- To be mindful of how their actions affect others
- To show how many people of different ethnicities and races are impacted by racism

(Continued)

(Continued)

MATERIALS

- Students' cell phones (optional)
- Computer with internet and speakers
- Magazines or e-magazines

Session Outline

What Are We Doing Today?

We are learning about how we are affected by racism and how stereotypes influence how we think about ourselves and other people.

Review It

Time: 5–10 minutes

Write the following questions in two areas of the room. As the students walk in, have them immediately write their answers below the questions:

- How did the adults you complimented respond? Are adults impacted by standards of appearance the same way young people can be?
- Did you check out the toys or games? What connections did you make about what we discussed in the last session and the toys and games you have in your life?

ACTIVITY: What's Your Favorite?

Time: 10 minutes

Purpose: To have students share their favorite media so they can link the media they consume with an ability to analyze it for race bias

To set the stage and get kids comfortable with the subject of media use, do a "gallery walk" of their favorite media. In different areas of the room write TV Shows, Movies, Games, *and* Websites/Magazines. *Then ask the students to walk around with markers and write their answers for each category.*

- What magazines do you read?
- What websites do you check out most often?
- What video games do you play?
- What are your favorite TV shows?
- What are your favorite movies?

Debrief

Are there patterns to the responses? If so, can you describe them?

Takeaways

We are going to examine what the media you see most often are communicating to you.

ACTIVITY: Seeing the Hidden Messages

Time: 30 minutes (15 minutes for exercise and 10–15 minutes for debrief)

Purpose: To show students the hidden messages about race in the media they consume

Divide the students into small groups. Say: Last session we learned about gender expectations and messages you receive about how boys and girls are supposed to look. This session, we will further our understanding by examining how people of different races and ethnicities appear in magazines, websites, video/mobile games, TV shows, and movies. We will look for and analyze the "unwritten" messages or codes in these forms of media. To do this, each group will receive questions to research and discuss regarding one of the media areas we just walked around the room to answer. For example, one group will answer the questions relating to movies; another group will answer the questions connected to websites and magazines. As you do your research together, one person in the group will write down your most important findings. Then we will come back together as one group, and one person from each group will report your insights. To find your answers, you can also use Wikipedia or a search engine and look up images. Or if you have TV or movies, you can visit the website imdb.com.

Hand out the following questions:

- Does your media area have people/characters of different races or ethnicities?
- If it does, what are the characters doing?
- If your media area has main characters, what race/ethnicity is the main protagonist or hero/heroine? What race is the enemy or villain?
- Are there any sidekicks? If so, what race are they?
- What are the top five characteristics that come to mind to describe the person (or people) of color you see?
- Did any of these images confirm or challenge a racial or ethnic stereotype?
- What unwritten codes or messages are conveyed in these images?

Debrief

Before we ask people to share their group's answer, first let's talk about how it felt to answer those questions. Was it ever uncomfortable? Why?

Have a student from each group share his or her insights, allowing for students from other groups to ask questions or make additional comments.

Takeaways

Talking about these topics can be uncomfortable. But if we don't talk about them, we mindlessly absorb the meanings behind these images.

ACTIVITY: How the Appearance Boxes Fit

THINK ABOUT IT

Time: 15 minutes

Purpose: To connect race and ethnic stereotypes with gender/appearance stereotypes

Show the appearance boxes the group created last session. If you don't have the boxes, ask the students to say five things they remember from last session about each box. Say: Last week we made boxes that showed how there can be expectations of how we look.

I'm going to give you a few minutes in your group to go back to the images you viewed. Look at how people of color—both men and women—are depicted in the images you saw and compare them to the standards of appearance we discussed in the last session. In your groups, ask each other the following questions:

If we combine the boy box with the messages we see about boys and men of particular races, what assumptions and messages are communicated in those images?

- What are the messages you can see about being an African American boy or man? How do they express their anger? Affection? Courage?
- What are the messages you can see about being a Latino boy or man? How do they express their anger? Affection? Courage?
- What are the messages you can see about being an Asian boy or man? How do they express their anger? Affection? Courage?

If we combine the girl box with the messages we see about women and girls of particular races, what assumptions and messages are communicated in those images?

- What are the messages you can see about being an African American girl or woman? How do they express their anger? Affection? Courage?
- What are the messages you can see about being a Latina girl or woman? How do they express their anger? Affection? Courage?
- What are the messages you can see about being an Asian girl or woman? How do they express their anger? Affection? Courage?

Look at the images again. Do any of the minorities look like they changed their appearance to get closer to the white standard of beauty? (straightened hair, lightened skin, eye surgery for Asian women, etc.)

- Why do you think people do this?
- What is gained, in your view? What is lost?

Say: Different people experience the same media images differently. If you are white and seeing these images of people of color, then it's easy to absorb these messages and believe them without thinking about them. If you are the race of the people in these images, what are the possible emotions you could feel? You can feel angry, frustrated, or not seen for who you are.

Debrief

How do you think you would feel if people who weren't your race treated you like you were similar to these images?

Takeaways

You can feel like you can't act ever like that image because then you are conforming to a negative stereotype. It's really confusing! But what's not confusing is that people are affected by these issues, and these messages stop people from seeing others for who they are.

ACTIVITY: Get It Out

Time: 20 minutes

Purpose: To express feelings about the session topics

It's natural to have feelings about these topics, no matter what race or ethnicity you are. Here are two video examples of people sharing their feelings. Let's watch them, and then take a few minutes to get our own feelings out. The first video is of a Japanese spoken-word artist. The second video is about letting go of labels we put on ourselves and others.

https://youtu.be/61lLSroXh6U

https://youtu.be/q0qD2K2RWkc

Let's stand up, jump up and down, then close our eyes and take five deep breaths. Then I'll hand out some paper and you can draw how you're feeling or write a poem. If you want to share what you drew or wrote, we can do that too.

Debrief

What emotions did you see in those videos?

Takeaways

When you have strong emotions—feel passionately or even overwhelmed—it's good to express them somehow.

Wrap It Up

Time: 5 minutes

- These are really hard topics to discuss. It can feel overwhelming and uncomfortable.
- There doesn't have to be an answer beyond "dignity isn't negotiable."
- You aren't a bad person for having racist assumptions and beliefs. We all live in this culture, so we all have been influenced by these messages.
- But now that we know, we have a responsibility to be aware when we are saying or doing something because of these assumptions.
- Remember: If you make a mistake you can always go back to that person and apologize.
- Please tell your parent/guardian or an adult to whom you are close what we discussed in today's session. Tell them one thing you thought was most important and why. If they disagree with what you're saying, ask them why.

Carry It With You

Listen to your playlist, or listen to what your friends are sharing with you. What messages do you get from the lyrics? If a certain song/artist stands out to you, look at the video and examine what the images are communicating. What are the codes/unwritten messages they are sending? Be prepared to discuss them next session.

Facing Race, Ethnicity, and Gender

Did I Say Something Wrong?

This session builds from the last and challenges students to think about how racial and gender stereotypes affect their lives and the lives of their peers. Because the nature of this session is personal, be aware of the student demographics and classroom dynamics in your room and consider how they might affect how students respond to the content. For example, if you have a majority of white students and a small number of black, Latino, or Asian students, be careful that the minority students don't feel they have to represent their racial or ethnic group. One way to imagine how they may feel is to pretend it is the seventh grade and there is only one girl in a group of guys, and the teacher is talking about girls getting their periods. How might that topic in that classroom dynamic make her feel? Or imagine there is only one boy in a group of girls and the teacher is explaining how boys get erections. How might that topic in that classroom dynamic make him feel? Everyone thinks the one minority member is the expert because they're the only person in the room who represents the group the teacher is discussing. They're the "expert" girl or the "expert" boy, so it's easy for them to feel extremely self-conscious. For students who are in the racial minority in a class, that dynamic can be even more intense because they are having similar experiences outside the classroom as well.

So why talk about these issues? Middle school kids are figuring out who they are—socially, emotionally, academically, culturally, and racially. It's all about digging into identity. And with that identity work, middle school students can be supportive yet cruel, selfless yet selfish, and idealistic yet racist at the same time.

OBJECTIVES

- To understand how cultural appropriation impacts various minority groups
- To understand that asking questions about race and ethnic difference is not inherently racist; being genuinely curious about someone else's life experience and history is a good thing

(Continued)

(Continued)

- To create a learning environment where making a mistake and saying something "wrong" or out of curiosity and a desire to learn will be accepted by others
- To appreciate the complexities and pressures any minority student may feel being the only one who represents a group of people
- To incorporate SEAL into thinking about how to address racism and bigotry

MATERIALS

- Students' cell phones (optional)
- Computer with internet and speakers

Session Outline

What Are We Doing Today?

We are learning about why people react in certain ways to what we say about race, ethnicity, and gender.

Review It

Time: 10 minutes

Last session's Carry It With You was about listening to your favorite playlists and maybe seeing images differently. First, each of us (including me, because I did the assignment as well) will write down anything that stood out for us. Second, I want you to write on the board a word or phrase that best summarizes your thoughts and feelings about what you wrote down. Or we can watch one of the videos we viewed at the end of the session.

ACTIVITY: Cultural Appropriation

Time: 20–25 minutes

Purpose: To teach students how easy it can be to be ignorant of other cultures, and to become more aware of the consequences

Ask: Who remembers how we have defined culture? How do you show your culture?

Cultural appropriation is the adoption or use of elements of one culture by members of a different culture.

Ask (and have students write responses individually or in small groups): What are some Halloween costumes you've worn or seen others wear? Now, we're going to look at one way to "see" certain types of costumes.

For sixth and seventh graders: a short video of Native American people trying on "Indian" Halloween costumes and discussing their feelings about the costumes and their culture: https://youtu.be/frX69E9pkf8

For eighth graders: Amandla Stenberg, "Don't Cash Crop on My Cornrows": https://youtu.be/O1KJRRSB_XA

Debrief for Sixth and Seventh Graders

- What are examples of other types of costumes that are similar to those we saw in the video?
- What are good examples of costumes? Why?
- Can you think of other common costumes that depict other groups of people in similar ways to what we saw in the video?

Debrief for Eighth Graders

- What do you believe is the most important takeaway from the video? Why?
- Why do you think people might not take the video seriously?
- Is there anything you heard with which you disagreed? Why?
- As in other sessions, we have discussed that when a person is offended or hurt, they are entitled to their feelings. No one has the right to tell them they are wrong about what they think or feel. But remember, it can be hard to talk about being offended for all the reasons we have discussed in earlier sessions. Can someone remind me what those reasons are?

Takeaways

- As in the case of artists you like, you can still critique specific things they do. No one is usually all good or all bad.
- Someone's culture is not your costume. What does that mean now that we've checked out these videos?

ACTIVITY: Are You Really Asking a Question?

Time: 15 minutes

Purpose: To differentiate a curious question from a question that undermines or disrespects someone based on race

THINK ABOUT IT

It's great to hang out with people from different races and backgrounds than yours. When you do, it's natural that you may be genuinely curious about them—but you may also be worried that if you ask a question you may come across as being racist. So, we are going to think about how to tell the difference.

An example of a curious question shows that you really want to understand something about another person. Examples of curious questions are . . .

"What does your family have for Easter/Thanksgiving dinner?"

"Do you get sunburned?" (said to someone with dark skin)

"Where are you from?" (as opposed to "Are you Mexican?")

A fake curious question is a way to put someone down or make a racist or bigoted statement but hide it in a question. Examples of a fake curious question are . . .

"But where are you *really* from?"

"Why can *all* black people dance?"

"Why does your hair do *that*? Can I touch your hair?"

"Do you know someone who's been shot?"

"Why are all Asian students math geniuses?"

"Why are you all so angry all the time?"

"Do you have a dad?"

If you're a member of a minority and people are asking you questions about your racial and cultural identity, at times it can feel good to share your history with others. However, it can also be really annoying and make you angry if you feel like you constantly have to teach the people around you not to be so ignorant. Usually, people in those situations try to blow off the hurtful or ignorant comments for all the reasons we discussed in earlier sessions. But sometimes you lose your temper, and then people don't understand why you're so angry—and then you risk being the angry (insert minority) person. An occasional outburst in this situation is a normal human response; unfortunately, it can also contribute to racial stereotypes surrounding anger.

If you're accused of being racist and you really don't understand why, don't shut down. As uncomfortable as it may feel, ask the person who said that to you why your words or actions came across as racist because you really want to know.

ACTIVITY: What Do You Say?

THINK ABOUT IT

Time: 15 minutes

Purpose: To have students practice how to listen and discuss common race-oriented topic scenarios

Break the group into smaller groups, and give them the following scenarios. They have to discuss the possible feelings of the different people in the scenario and then use SEAL to think through how to address the problem.

You're of Chinese background and your friends are constantly making little comments about Asians that really irritate you. But the comments are all technically positive, like how smart all Asians are and how they're going to get into the best schools. How do you talk to them about it?

Your family is Hispanic and has lived in this country for a long time. There are kids in your English class who make "jokes" by asking you when you're going to go back to your country.

You are African American and have a white friend who uses the *n*-word. You eventually tell him to stop but he asks, "Why can you say the '*n*-word' but I can't? You know I'm not a racist."

Debrief

What was the most frustrating issue for the subject of the scenario? What strategies did your group come up with to address these frustrations?

Takeaways

Regardless of the racial/ethnic background of the subject in these scenarios, it's always challenging to know when and what to say. You don't want to "make too much" of the problem, and you don't want it to seem like what they're doing really bothers you.

ACTIVITY: It Shouldn't All Be on One Person's Shoulders

THINK ABOUT IT

Time: 15 minutes

Purpose: To build from the last activity and show how much pressure individual students feel to speak out and build empathy in the other students so they have more incentive to support the minority student

Write on the board:

My friends all know how much I hate the *n*-word, especially since they're white. My friends and I were walking down the street and we ran into another group of kids I knew and one of them (a white boy) came up to me and said, "What's up, my *n* . . . ?" I was furious, but my friends said I was overreacting. ("Winston")

Debrief

- Do you think Winston was right to be angry? Why? Why not?
- Why do you think Winston's friends told him he was overreacting?

- In other sessions, the issue of people being told they were overreacting has come up. Where has that happened, and who was told that? Do you see any connections?
- What do you think Winston would have wanted his friends to do instead?

Takeaways

- Winston shouldn't feel like he has to stand up to this bigoted comment all by himself.
- Winston's friends need to appreciate that they should back him up—not by fighting the other guy but by agreeing with Winston and supporting his right to speak his truth.
- Many of us have been or will be in situations where we are told to be quiet. We need our friends to support us in those moments.

(Instructor note: You may have an African American student in the room who says she doesn't mind if her friend uses the n-word because that person has somehow earned the right to say it. In the words of one of our favorite Owning Up *educators, Shanterra McBride, "I am offended by the word because of its history of violence and hate. I'm thinking about the student of color who would want to not ruffle feathers or shake it off even if there are other African American students who are offended by it. I think it's important to acknowledge that even though young people hear the n-word so often in certain types of music, or there may be reasons why they think certain people can say that word while others can't, neither of those facts takes away from its history and use to dehumanize African American people.")*

ACTIVITY: Listen to the Words

Time: 15 minutes

Purpose: To use song lyrics to help students analyze race privilege behavior and self-reflect on their own behavior

Have the group listen to the first part of the song "White Privilege II" by Macklemore, from "Pulled into the parking lot" to "Or should I stand on the side and shut my mouth?" (http://genius.com/Macklemore-and-ryan-lewis-white-privilege-ii-lyrics).

Debrief/Takeaways

- What do you think is the most important thing he is saying?
- Can you describe why he is confused about what to do?
- If you're white, what do you think is the best way to show your defiance of racism?

ACTIVITY: Let's Share Our Stories

Time: 20 minutes

Purpose: To challenge the students to own up to their experiences with racism

Give each student a piece of paper and a pen and ask them to sit by themselves wherever they want in the room (except near a close friend). Ask them to write, anonymously, their answer to the questions you are about to ask them. Give them 5 to 10 minutes to answer, then collect the papers. Next, have all the students sit in a circle and ask them not to look at one another while you read their responses aloud. Then ask them to share their thoughts after hearing their peers' answers.

Say: I am going to give you a choice to answer one of three questions:

1. Have you ever heard someone say something racist? It could have been a joke, or they could have been serious. When you noticed it, do you remember how you felt?

2. Has someone ever said something racist to you? How did you feel? How did you react? If you could go back to that moment, is there anything you would like to change about the way you responded?

3. Now that we've talked about this issue a bit, is there something that you've done or said that you acknowledge could have been racist? What was it, and did you realize it at the time?

Debrief

- How did you feel answering the question?
- How does it feel listening to other students in the class share their stories?
- Is there something another person in the class shared that you could relate to, or do you want to say something to support them?

Takeaways

Just like we talked about last session, discussing these issues can be uncomfortable, but it's worth doing. You aren't a bad person for having racist assumptions and beliefs. We all live in this culture, so we all have been influenced by these messages.

Wrap It Up

Time: 5 minutes

- If you make a mistake you can always go back to that person and apologize.
- When you are curious about someone or something about them, ask them in a respectful way.
- You can have really uncomfortable conversations and learn from them!

Carry It With You

Is there a situation going on with people you know right now where you could apply what we have discussed in the session today and make someone feel more supported? If you can't think of anything now, take that question home and carry it with you.

Finding Support

Don't Go It Alone

Many young people assume that going to adults is "snitching" or weak and will make a problem worse. This session challenges that belief and encourages students both to seek and to give support. That being said, it is critical to acknowledge that students may have had experiences with adults who were supposed to support them and didn't, or who even exacerbated the problem. But not all adults are like that, and this session's goal is to focus on the adults who truly can be helpful.

OBJECTIVES

- To help students identify their support network and encourage them to work to strengthen the relationships that help them
- To examine reasons why it can be difficult to ask for help and support
- To help students learn how to give one another supportive advice
- To help students identify allies

MATERIALS

- Index cards
- Pencils or pens

Session Outline

What Are We Doing Today?

We are learning where and how to ask for help in a way that makes the situation better.

Review It

Time: 5 minutes

What did you carry with you from the last session?

ACTIVITY: Are You Giving or Getting Good Advice?

THINK ABOUT IT

Time: 15 minutes

Purpose: To have students self-reflect on how they may give and receive advice

Raise your hand if you . . .

- Have you ever tried to give someone advice and they wouldn't take it?
- Had someone get angry with you when you tried to help them?

Now I want you to think of a time when someone gave you advice that you thought was really annoying. It could have been a friend, a person in your family, a teacher, a coach, or even a random person. Do you remember specifically what they said or how they said it that you didn't like?

Give three examples of getting advice about friends, grades, teachers, or problems with parents or siblings that you found really annoying:

1.

2.

3.

Now give three examples of someone giving you advice that made you want to listen:

1.

2.

3.

- What are phrases or words someone could use that would make it easier for you to listen to them?
- How could the person who gave you annoying advice have gotten through to you in a way that you would have listened and accepted their help?
- Looking back on the situation where the person got mad at you for giving them advice, do you have any ideas why they resisted you?

So when you give advice, you are going to focus on these three things . . .

1.

2.

3.

ACTIVITY: Your Support Network

Time: 15 minutes

Purpose: To have students define their own personal support network

The definition of *support* comes from the Latin, a combination of *sub* ("from below") and *portare* ("to carry"). Let's brainstorm so you have your own personal definition of support.

Explain that people who help you form a support network. Give each student two index cards and ask them to draw their support network as it existed last year or six months ago on one card, then as it exists now on the other.

Debrief

- What are the strengths of your support networks, then and now?
- Could you make your support network stronger? How?
- Have you ever really wanted to ask someone for help but didn't? What stopped you?
- Have you ever resisted someone who was trying to help you even though you really needed and wanted their help? If so, why?

Takeaways

Everyone needs a support network: a map in their heads of who is the best person to listen when they're going through a hard situation, to give advice when they ask it of them, and sometimes to tell them when they need to look at their behavior or think in a different way.

ACTIVITY: Advice Situations

Time: 20 minutes

Purpose: To teach students to give supportive advice in a variety of situations from an advice-column perspective

You write an advice column for your school paper. For example, a seventh grader writes to you for help because a friend is getting other people to gang up on her. Choose one of the following scenarios. Using SEAL and other information you've learned in this program, how would you advise her to work out her problem?

1. I know my friend is mad at me, but she won't admit it to my face. Instead, she ignores me and is really fake. What do I do?

2. My friend is always trying to copy me. It's really weird. I try telling her to get her own style, but she doesn't change. Now I feel like she's forcing me to be mean to her. What do I do?

3. I'm so worried about everything—school, friends, my family. I feel really over-whelmed, but I don't know how to talk about it. I don't even know the words to say to explain it. Sometimes I just want to disappear. How do I get these feelings to go away?

4. Most people at school seem to have more money than me. There's no way my parents can afford half the things a lot of the students have at this school. It makes me angry.

5. I have a friend who is obsessed about her weight. She throws up regularly after she eats. I've told her she's not fat, but nothing I do or say changes anything. Now I'm starting to have doubts about my own body and wonder if I'm fat too. What can I do to help her and myself?

6. I know my boyfriend is treating me badly in front of other people, but when I confront him he won't admit it. But he's really nice to me other times. Should I dump him?

7. My parents are always on my case about school and homework. They constantly tell me how lazy I am. Sometimes I get so angry with them I yell and slam my door, and then they won't listen to the reason why I got so mad in the first place. I don't know how to talk to them anymore. How do I talk to them without blow-ing up or shutting down?

8. My BFF has turned on me and is getting other people not to talk to me. I don't know what I did wrong. What should I do?

Debrief

Ask a student from each group to share their advice. As they do, emphasize what they discussed in the earlier exercise. Were they following their own advice about how to communicate in these situations?

Takeaways

Good advice makes the person feel like they been listened to, acknowledged, and given a way to think through the problem that is realistic.

ACTIVITY: Girls Supporting Girls and Guys Supporting Guys

Time: 15 minutes

Purpose: To connect issues of support with same-sex interactions and friendships

If a girl says, "I don't trust other girls" or "I just can't talk to girls" . . .

Ask the following questions:

- What would make a girl feel this way about other girls?

- What is the best way to get a girl who doesn't trust other girls to change her mind—to believe that some girls are worthy of her trust?

- If you knew a girl who didn't trust other girls, what could you do to strengthen your friendship with her?

If a guy says, "There's no way I can talk to my friends about a problem I'm having because they'll just make fun of me or blow me off" . . .

Ask the following questions:

- What would make a guy feel this way about other guys?

- What is the best way to get a guy to change his mind—to believe he can trust other guys with his problems?

- If you knew a guy who didn't trust other people, what could you do to strengthen your friendship with him?

- If you are a guy who doesn't trust other guys, why would it be worth it to risk trusting someone?

Debrief

How do you think not trusting people in these situations can affect someone?

Takeaways

Making assumptions about not being able to trust a group of people, even if those people look like they have a lot in common with you, makes it harder to have friendships you can count on, and it makes it harder for you to be a good friend.

ACTIVITY: Being an Ally

Time: 15 minutes

Purpose: To have students identify at least one adult in their life who can offer advice and support

Everyone needs at least one adult ally, if at all possible. In general, this is someone you can go to for help, advice, and feedback, even if some of it is hard to hear. But it's important to come up with your own criteria—the things you need—for your ally.

I'm going to hand each of you a piece of paper. You'll have a few minutes to come up with three to five words that describe your personal definition of *ally*.

Now I want you think of at least one person in your life who can be this ally for you. You don't have to be close to this person right now. You could barely know them. You could decide through this exercise that they are someone you think would be good to have on your side. Write down their name.

Debrief/Takeaways

Now that you have decided on that person, if you have a problem that's really confusing or overwhelming, you already know who you can go to for advice. It's one less decision you have to make. Plus, you'll have made the decision when you were calm and focused, and not freaking out with anxiety.

Wrap It Up

Time: 5 minutes

- Sometimes an ally's support will come in the form of telling you things you don't want to hear.
- It's common to have problems that are too big to handle by yourself. You are demonstrating a skill when you can recognize that you need to get someone else involved.
- Put your support network in a private place (maybe where you have placed your Friendship Bill of Rights), where you can refer to it whenever you need it.

Carry It With You

Remember the adult you identified as an ally? If you don't feel comfortable telling that person you've chosen them as an ally, put their name in a private place (in your phone's notes or memo app, for example). That way you're more likely to remember this person when you are in a situation where you need support.

Crushes and Rejection

SESSION

14

Do They Like Me?

Is there anything more confusing for older children and teens than sorting out their feelings when they "like" someone? It can be especially stressful in middle school, when all of a kid's romantic ups and downs are often played out in public and their friends can observe, comment, and interfere. This has always been the case in adolescence, but it has never been more so than today, with social media.

While adults often describe these relationships as "puppy love," these experiences are important to our students, and the social norms young people learn in their early relationships are profound. They set behavior patterns for how young people communicate their needs and boundaries later in their lives. Moreover, as any middle school educator knows, if your students are preoccupied with some kind of relationship drama, it's significantly more challenging to get anything done in class.

A note about how to approach this topic: We try to avoid using the term *intimate relationships* to describe relationships with possible or existing romantic/sexual interactions among any of our students. We do this because we want to stress that relationships without such aspects can be and often are intimate. It is also crucial that every student feels that the session is designed to acknowledge his or her perspective and experience. This is not only connected to respecting differences in sexual orientation but also in physical development. We want all students to feel comfortable and included in this session, no matter where they are in their personal experience or physical development.

OBJECTIVES

- To create an accepting environment where students can discuss who they're attracted to and when they're attracted to other people
- To create an environment where students can recognize that everyone has different romantic preferences
- To understand the difference between being a supportive and interfering friend in other people's romantic interactions

(Continued)

(Continued)

- To affirm that young people can have romantic feelings and relationships that are important to them
- To connect earlier teaching modules about students' communicating personal boundaries in friendships with people they find attractive

MATERIALS

- Whiteboard
- Scenario handouts (one scenario per handout)

Session Outline
What Are We Doing Today?

We are learning how to think through some of the situations and complexities that occur when people like each other.

Review It

Time: 5 minutes

Last session we talked about giving advice and choosing an ally. Did anyone have a giving- or getting-advice situation occur between our last session and today that they want to discuss? Or did anyone come up with a new ally they hadn't considered before?

ACTIVITY: Talking About Crushes

Time: 10 minutes

Purpose: To create a learning environment about crushes and romantic feelings where every student feels included

Write in the middle of the board:

Crushes!

Above the word, write:

Some people . . .

Around the word, write:

> Have them a lot
>
> Sometimes
>
> Rarely
>
> Never

Say: In this session we are talking about when people like each other. The most important thing to remember about this topic is that people can feel different ways about liking people. And that means whatever you think about any of this is completely, totally acceptable because it's how you feel. For example, some people had their first crush when they were 5 years old, other people haven't felt that way about a person yet, and others might not ever feel that way. Some people are attracted to someone of the same sex, and some people are attracted to someone of the opposite sex. Some people get over a person in a day. Some people don't get over someone they like for a really long time. Some people really want girlfriends or boyfriends, and other people are completely uninterested in such relationships. Whatever describes you is exactly where you should be because it's how you feel. Your feelings can change too. You're figuring it out and so is everyone around you. But all this figuring out means that people can get really nervous and awkward about this topic. So if we need to take a break, that's totally okay.

ACTIVITY: How Does It Feel to Really Like Someone?

Time: 10 minutes

Purpose: To allow students to express the feelings they have when they like someone in a way that protects their privacy and also shows how they share similar feelings

Hand out index cards and pens.

Say: Put all the words that come to your mind that best describe what it feels like when you really like someone.

Collect the index cards and write the responses on the board.

Debrief

- Did we forget any words we need to add?
- How does it feel to get all these words out?
- Can people tell when a person has a crush or likes someone?
- Why do people like to get involved with "who likes whom"?

Takeaways

- Looking at all these words, it seems that liking someone or having a crush can make you feel great, terrible, and confused.

- You can't help what people you have crushes on.

- Sometimes people want to get involved in other people's love lives because it's a way for them to figure out all this stuff without having to go through it themselves.

ACTIVITY: Supportive Friends

Time: 15 minutes

Purpose: To make distinctions between being supportive or intrusive (and potentially spreading gossip and conflict) when a friend is attracted to someone

Say: People can get really involved in their friends' love lives. Sometimes that's a good thing, and sometimes it's not. So let's define the difference. I am going to split you into two groups. One group will give examples of what a supportive friend does when you like someone; the other group will give examples of what a nonsupportive friend does when you like someone.

When you like someone, a supportive friend . . .

- Tells you when you are being used or not being treated nicely by the person you like
- Makes you feel better if you're feeling insecure
- Tells you the relationship isn't good for you in a way that doesn't make you feel stupid
- Talks/comments/posts about this part of your life

When you like someone, a nonsupportive friend . . .

- Makes you choose between the person you like and your friends
- Makes you feel stupid for liking the person you like
- Tells you the relationships isn't good for you in a way that makes you feel stupid
- Talks/comments/posts about this part of your life

Debrief

Can you share an example of someone being a supportive friend?

Takeaways

Sometimes people have friends they really like who have lots of good qualities but who are not supportive in this area. You have to decide how important having a supportive friend is to you.

ACTIVITY: This Stuff Is So Complicated!

Time: 20 minutes

Purpose: To apply the ideas just covered to realistic situations

Break into small groups. Each group is given a scenario where they have to discuss the questions and come up with a strategy. They can demonstrate their strategy with a role play, a poem, or an infographic they can draw.

> **Scenario 1: Betrayal.** Elena has been hanging out with Patrick for the past two weeks. Things are going well, but then Elena's friend tells her she saw Patrick getting together with another girl after school. Elena decides to confront him, but she can't decide how.

Discuss the following questions.

- How does the Act Like a Girl Box influence the way girls communicate in these situations?
- How does the Act Like a Boy Box influence the way boys communicate in these situations?
- How do girls usually show their anger in these situations? Is it effective?
- Do girls in this situation usually get angry with the guy or the other girl? If they do, why?

> **Scenario 2: The Blowup.** Charlie is hanging out with Dylan. Charlie really likes him, but Dylan can take a really long time to text back. Furthermore, around their friends, Dylan isn't very affectionate. At first, Charlie tries not to be bothered by it, but little by little it gets harder. It feels like Dylan is leading Charlie on. The next time Charlie sees Dylan, Charlie is obviously angry but Dylan ignores it. Charlie can't take it anymore and blows up, but Dylan gets mad at Charlie for blowing up.

Discuss the following questions.

- Why would Charlie blow up?
- What is "it" that Charlie can't take?
- What would other people in the group do when they saw the blowup?
- Is Dylan hoping that Charlie will keep quiet? Why?

> **Scenario 3: Rejection.** Alex has been hanging out with Carrie. Things have been going really well, but then Alex's friend tells him that Carrie likes someone else. Alex asks Carrie what's going on, and she says nothing is wrong.

Then she starts to avoid him. However, a little while later she texts him, so he thinks things between them are good. Then a friend tells him she hooked up with someone else. He feels devastated and embarrassed.

Debrief

- What are the most common ways people show they have just been rejected?
- What's the best way to tell someone you don't like them anymore?
- When Alex finds out that Carrie hooked up with someone else, what is the most likely thing he will do? Why?
- Will Alex reach out to his friends and tell any of them how upset he is? Why or why not?

Takeaways

Breaking up with someone should be clear, respectful, and private before you start with someone else. It's taking care of your business in a classy way.

Scenario 4: The Messy Break-Up. Mike and Annie are in the seventh grade and have been together for a few months. They share a big group of friends. Mike decides there are things that Annie does that he really doesn't like. She can be mean to people outside their group, and sometimes she doesn't treat him well. He breaks up with her as nicely as he can, but it's awkward. The break-up draws out for weeks, and other people in their group get involved.

Debrief

- What are the possible motivations for the friends to get involved in the break-up?
- What should Mike do if Annie's friends get mad at him for the break-up?
- If the girls accuse Mike of being conceited, are they right?

Takeaways

- People may accuse you of being conceited or mean, but if you treat the other person with dignity during the break-up, you owe no explanation to that person's friends.
- You have the right to disconnect from people who don't treat others (including you) with dignity.

Wrap It Up

Time: 5 minutes

- Whatever you feel about liking or being attracted to someone is acceptable because they're your feelings.
- Everyone is allowed to be hurt when people end relationships with them. It's not weak to feel bad.

- Whatever you feel about liking people, your friends can feel differently. It's also true that if you are in relationship that you think is bad for you, you have the right to end it. You are all going through this together—even though it might not feel that way at times.

Carry It With You

If you hear gossip about someone's crush or rejections between this session and the next, ask what story or assumptions you are telling yourself about the people or the situation.

Recognizing and Respecting Boundaries

How Far Is Too Far?

While it's true that some young people in middle school hesitate to hold hands with each other, or aren't yet sexually interested in others, some of our students are in situations where issues of consent are appropriate. While respecting the different developmental levels of our students, it is clear that the perceived or real sexual experiences of some students can affect interactions between students as well as among the overall student culture.

This session is built to age-appropriately connect the earlier sessions on boundaries in friendships, the difficulty in communicating those boundaries with friends, and the influence of cultural messages to direct how young people believe they should behave in hooking up, dating, or any kind of sexually intimate relationships.

OBJECTIVES

- To affirm young people's right to express themselves
- To respectfully discuss issues of personal boundaries in sexual interactions in a manner where all students feel included in the content and possible discussion
- To affirm young people's right to privacy
- To help young people create their own personal boundaries
- To demonstrate the value of clearly communicating personal boundaries

MATERIALS

- Computer with audio and screen

Session Outline

What Are We Doing Today?

Today's session will cover how people can struggle to tell what they want or don't want in their personal relationships with people they like and/or are attracted to.

Review It

> **Time:** 5–10 minutes

Last session's Carry It With You was about what happens when you overhear or people try to get you involved in gossip about people's crushes and rejections. I am not going to ask you if that happened to you, because that's private information. But I do want to know what gossip you heard on social media about public figures that you think fits what we discussed during our last session.

ACTIVITY: Who Made the Mistake?

THINK ABOUT IT

> **Time:** 20–30 minutes
>
> **Purpose:** To show how the dynamics of technology, flirting, and group dynamics can combine to hurt and isolate people

Roll a die to see which scenario to do with your students first.

Scenario: What Does It Mean to Win? Ashley really likes Connor, and she's been flirting with him at school and online. One of Connor's friends tells Ashley that a girl at another school really likes him too. Ashley is really nervous about this other girl taking Connor away from her. So on a Friday night when she gets back from practice, she's in her room Snapchatting with Connor and she decides to take a selfie in her bra and send it to him. Ashley doesn't know that Connor has two friends sleeping over at his house that night, and that when he receives the picture he shares it with them. One of the boys manages to save the picture and then sends it to their other friends.

Debrief

- Does Ashley have a right to send pictures of herself like that to Connor without asking his permission first?
- Does Connor have an obligation to protect her privacy so other people don't see the photo?
- Is there an unspoken rule that Connor needs to send a picture back?
- Let's say Ashley is really upset because she wanted only Connor to see the picture. If you were Ashley's friend and people were posting or saying mean things about her, what do you think would be the best way you could support her?

- Which one is the worse problem: taking and sending the picture, or receiving the picture and then sharing it with other people without asking their permission first? If you think they're equally bad, why?

Takeaways

- You have the right to make a "mistake" of trusting someone who then violates your privacy, and not to have them or anybody else make fun of you.

- Just because someone says a person "was just doing it for attention" doesn't mean they wanted attention from everyone.

- Someone's possible or real embarrassment should not be entertaining.

Scenario: Is Anything Wrong? Ben sends a picture of himself getting out of the shower to his friend, David, with the hashtag "#so hot." A towel is covering the lower half of his body. David tells people at school that Ben was hitting on him. Other people start harassing Ben about being gay.

Debrief

- Did anyone do anything wrong in this situation? If so, why?

- If Ben is flirting with David, are his actions any different from Ashley's sending a similar picture to Connor?

- If Ben sent the same picture to a girl, how do you think other students would react?

- Both Ashley and Ben sent a sexual picture to someone. Should their actions be judged equally?

Takeaways

If you send a picture of yourself that people use to embarrass you, here's a suggested response:

> I regret sending that picture because people violated my trust. Your bringing it up makes me feel worse. I promise you I never would have tried to make you feel bad if you were in my shoes. I don't want to talk about this anymore with you.

Scenario: Out of Control PDA. Jett and Grace are a couple. In passing periods and lunch, Grace likes to show him a lot of affection and wants him to reciprocate with equal amounts. She's always hugging him and sitting on his lap at lunch. Grace's displays of affection around other people make Jett uncomfortable.

Debrief

- Should Jett ever say anything to Grace about his feelings?

- How do you think someone in Grace's position usually responds when she's told to stop publicly showing her boyfriend affection?

- What stops Jett from saying anything to her?
- In addition to telling her, what are other ways Jett could communicate to Grace how he feels?
- What if the roles were reversed and Grace were the one who didn't like the public displays of affection? Would any of your answers change?

Takeaways

- Even people in a relationship can change their minds about what they do and don't like doing with their partner. For example, on Monday one person in the couple may like hugging in front of all their friends and on Tuesday prefer not to.
- It can be hard to tell someone you like or are in a relationship with that you don't like something they're doing.
- People don't want to be uptight or make too much out of a problem, so they don't say anything or they communicate what they want unclearly.
- But in these situations, if someone you are attracted to or are in a relationship with pushes past what you feel comfortable doing with them, you have the right to say no, and you have the right to be listened to by your partner. Remember the definition of listening—*to be prepared to be changed by what you hear.*

Scenario: Empty House. Lisa and Mark really like each other. Lisa's parents don't get home from work until 6:30 p.m., and one afternoon Lisa asks Mark to come over to her house so they can be alone together. Mark's parents don't approve of him going to people's houses when their parents aren't home. Lisa asks Mark to hang out with her after school at her house, and he decides to go.

Debrief

- If Mark is doing things with Lisa that he doesn't feel comfortable doing, what would stop Mark from telling her?
- If Lisa is doing things with Mark that she doesn't feel comfortable doing, what would stop Lisa from telling him?
- What would be specific examples of good personal boundaries for Mark?
- What would be specific examples of good personal boundaries for Lisa?

Takeaways

- Boys have the right to say no just like girls do.
- Before you are alone with someone you are attracted to, ask yourself what you feel comfortable doing with that person and what you don't feel comfortable doing with that person.
- Everyone has their own personal boundaries.

ACTIVITY: Watch the Video *Consent: It's as Simple as Tea*

Time: 20 minutes

Purpose: To show the dynamics of sexual consent in an age-appropriate but relatable manner

Show the video: https://youtu.be/pZwvrxVavnQ

Say: The video refers to the word *consent.* What does that word mean to you?

- What are the top three things this video is trying to convince you to believe?
- Was it successful?
- Why would people not believe what this video is trying to say?
- Do you think it's relevant for people your age to watch this video? Why?

Debrief

What do you think is the most important message in this video to remember?

Takeaways

People have the right to say no to doing things with other people, no matter what the situation or circumstances may be.

Wrap It Up

Time: 5 minutes

- You have the right to express your feelings about liking someone or wanting to get their attention.
- You have the right to privacy—if you share something about yourself, you have the right to assume it will be kept private.
- That being said, just because you have that right doesn't mean you can count on people to respect it.

Carry It With You

From now until the next session, watch for the subtle and obvious ways people communicate their consent to other people. It could be sharing food during lunch, joining a pickup game on a playground, how a person receives affection from another person, or what you see in the media. Observe people's body language, what they say, and their tone of voice. In what ways are people communicating that they are giving consent in these moments? If they don't want to give consent or permission, how are they communicating their feelings? Be ready to discuss next session.

Sexual Harassment

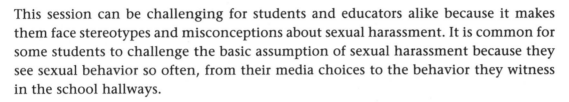

It's Complicated

SESSION
16

This session can be challenging for students and educators alike because it makes them face stereotypes and misconceptions about sexual harassment. It is common for some students to challenge the basic assumption of sexual harassment because they see sexual behavior so often, from their media choices to the behavior they witness in the school hallways.

Your students may approach this session with the following assumptions: (a) girls are the only targets of sexual harassment, (b) boys can't be sexually harassed, and/or (c) only boys can be sexual harassers. This session challenges those assumptions. It is about showing a larger context for understanding sexual harassment, explaining why it's so common for both boys and girls to send "mixed messages" when they're targeted, and providing tools to better read people's behavior and body language.

It is important to allow students to talk openly, even if they make comments that may be inappropriate or even incorrect. In response, challenge the students respectfully and provide facts. You may also have to remind them that they can say "inappropriate words" as long as they are used in an appropriate response to a question being asked.

As in Session 15, about consent, checking your own baggage is absolutely critical to achieving this session's goals. Reassure students that they can talk with you after the session if they have questions and concerns that they do not want to share with the group. If a student brings a concern to you in private that makes you feel uncomfortable or uncertain, reach out to the school's counselor, a social worker, or another professional.

OBJECTIVES

- To connect the concepts we covered in earlier sessions on sexual harassment; specifically, to link the prior topics of defining personal boundaries between friends—boundaries that can be very hard to communicate
- To define and describe different types of sexual harassment
- To help students recognize and respect their boundaries for wanted and unwanted sexual attention

(Continued)

(Continued)

- To challenge the assumption that all boys want all sexual attention from girls
- To help students become aware of harassment issues faced by lesbian, gay, bisexual, transgender, and questioning (LGBTQ) students
- To increase awareness that sexual harassment is against the law as well as against school policy, and to encourage students to report sexual harassment

MATERIALS

- Whiteboard or flip chart
- Index cards

CHECK YOUR BAGGAGE

- What experiences with sexual harassment did you have when you were young that inform your feelings to facilitate this information?
- Is there a student or group of students who could react to today's session in a way that would anger or frustrate you? What is the best way you can maintain being a calm, fair, and authoritative leader if they challenge you?

What Are We Doing Today?

Today we are learning about what sexual harassment really looks like to people your age and why it can be confusing to define and discuss.

Review It

Time: 5–10 minutes

Last session I asked you to observe how people give consent or permission to other people. I asked you how you knew, especially if the communication was more subtle— like the person communicated with body language or tone of voice. So if you observed something like that, can you describe the interaction?

ACTIVITY: Kahoot Exercise

Time: 5 minutes

Create an exercise on Kahoot (https://getkahoot.com) with the following responses. Ask the students to check if they agree with each of these statements.

1. People who sexually harass other people always know they're doing it.
2. People always feel flattered or like it when someone is flirting with them.
3. There is a federal law that protects students from harassment.
4. Boys can be sexually harassed.

As an alternative, you can ask the students to close their eyes and raise their hand if they agree with each of the above statements. For each statement, you will tally the number on the board.

Debrief

What was most interesting or surprising about people's responses?

Takeaways

The answers to the four questions are as follows: 1. No; 2. No; 3. Yes; 4. Yes

ACTIVITY: Types of Sexual Harassment

Time: 20 minutes

Purpose: To define *sexual harassment*

So what is sexual harassment? It can be one of those terms people say without thinking, but what it really means can be complicated and confusing. That being said, here's the definition we are going to use:

> Sexual harassment is unwanted and unwelcome sexual attention and behavior. Anyone can be a target of sexual harassment—adult or child, no matter what your gender. Anyone can also be a perpetrator of sexual harassment.

On the board or flip chart, write the categories Visual, Verbal/Written, *and* Physical *as column headings. Ask students to give examples. Categorize their responses as they do.*

Visual	Verbal/Written	Physical
Gesturing with hand or body	Comments and jokes	Pinching
Staring at body	Notes, drawings, pictures	Grabbing
Touching own body parts	Graffiti	Rubbing
Flashing or mooning	Sexual names	Brushing against you
Showing sexual photos	Homophobic comments	Pulling at/off clothing
	E-mails/ text messages/posts on social media with sexual content	Hugging/kissing

Debrief

Is everything on this list always sexual harassment?

No, sexual comments or flirting aren't always sexual harassment. But this is where it gets tricky: What one person may feel is acceptable may not be acceptable to another person. And just because the person was okay with it once doesn't automatically and forever mean they will always like the sexual attention.

Who defines it as sexual harassment?

The behavior is defined as sexual harassment by the person who is receiving it. If they don't like it and they see it as sexual harassment, then it is.

Why would a person not want to tell anyone about being sexually harassed?

There are many reasons why people don't like to tell. The most common are: (a) they don't want to make things uncomfortable with the other person; (b) they think people won't believe them; (c) they think the other person will use their power somehow to punish them; or (d) they think the behavior is normal, so it would be weird to complain.

Is there a difference between boys and girls not wanting to admit to being sexually harassed?

It can be really hard for girls when they're sexually harassed. It can happen in public places like walking down the street, the hallway, or among their friends. For some girls, it can feel like their physical safety is at risk. At the same time, people sometimes mistakenly believe that only girls or women can be targets of sexual harassment and that boys and men cannot be harassed because they always welcome sexual attention. Boys can be targets of sexual harassment, though they may not admit it because they're worried people might make fun of them, not believe them, or question their heterosexuality. So both boys and girls can be sexually harassed, and it's always serious.

Why do people do it even if they know the other person doesn't like it?

Possible answers:

- Because people think it's funny.
- A lot of people do it.
- It's not a big deal.
- They thought the person liked it.
- Their friends encouraged or pushed them to do it.

Where have we heard similar answers in other sessions?

In Session 3, the teasing section.

What are the consequences of being sexually harassed?

Sexual harassment can have a big impact on how safe or comfortable people feel at school and how they perform at school.

Can you give some examples?

- Avoid the person who bothered or harassed them.
- Talk less in class.
- Don't want to go to school.
- Change their seat in class to get farther away from someone.
- Find it hard to pay attention in school.
- Stay away from particular places in the school or on the school grounds.
- Find it hard to study.
- Lose their appetite or aren't interested in eating.
- Stay home from school or cut a class.
- Don't want to hang out with friends anymore.
- Prefer to be alone or work alone.

Takeaways

Sexual harassment can make people dread going to school, walking down the street, being in a class or group they love to participate in at school, or just going about their business.

ACTIVITY: SEAL Sexual Harassment Situations

Time: 20 minutes

Purpose: To connect the definition of *sexual harassment* with common situations

Break into small groups and read each of the following situations aloud (or choose however many your time allows). Ask whether each one is sexual harassment according to the definition you discussed. Choose one of the students to record the verdict on each one. Then take one of them that is labeled as sexual harassment and come up with a SEAL to confront the harasser (and remember to include the pushbacks). Keep the Act Like a Girl and Act Like a Boy Boxes in mind as you do this work, as well.

1. When a guy walks by a certain group of girls at school, they laugh, mess up his hair, and say something to him. He laughs and then walks away.
2. A guy in your class hugs a girl almost every time he sees her. She doesn't like it but doesn't say anything because she doesn't want to hurt his feelings.
3. A boy gives his girlfriend a shoulder massage in the hallway.
4. A girl tells a guy he's really hot.
5. A student tells an out male student that he looks really sexy today and he'd want to go out with him if he were a girl.

Say: Now let's report our verdicts to the overall group and have the following discussion. Where did your group agree and disagree?

If time permits, ask for volunteers to role-play each of the harassment situations, using the SEAL strategy. After each role play, encourage group discussion, including the following questions.

Debrief

- How does the Act Like a Girl Box influence the way a girl thinks about sexual harassment and her right to complain?
- How does the Act Like a Boy Box influence the way a boy thinks about sexual harassment and his right to complain?
- Is harassment that takes place on social media any different from harassment that takes place in person? If so, how?
- How do students feel about sexual harassment in your school? Do they think it is a problem, or do they think it is something normal and acceptable?

Takeaways

It's possible that a person may not intend to harass you. In order for a harasser to have the opportunity to change their behavior, you need to tell the person what the behavior is that you don't want and to ask for it to stop. At the same time, it can be really hard for some people to admit that they don't like the behavior. That's the case for both boys and girls because boys and girls are trained to avoid saying no, but for very different reasons. Girls get messages from the Act Like a Girl Box to be "nice" and not hurt people's feelings. Boys get messages from the Act Like a Boy Box that they have to like all sexual attention they get from girls. But if you don't like the attention someone is giving you, you have the right to be left alone.

Wrap It Up

Time: 5 minutes

- Sexual harassment can be hard to define because often the target doesn't want to seem uptight or hurt the other person's feelings. That's why it can be so hard for the target to communicate what he or she doesn't like. SEAL gives you a road map to articulate your feelings.
- Sexual harassment is a two-way street. The target needs to give the harasser the chance to know how his or her behavior is received and to change that behavior. But the harasser shouldn't take advantage of how uncomfortable the situation is.

Carry It With You

Write on the board *Words in Your Head*. As you walk out of the session today, write a word on the board that most accurately describes what you are thinking right now.

Concluding the Program

Please Say You Learned Something!

This session offers students the opportunity to reflect on their experiences in the program and a forum for addressing their questions and concerns. Be prepared to hear their honest reactions to the questions you ask about how they view the sessions. If you listen carefully, you will come away with valuable insights into how to improve the program.

OBJECTIVES

- To encourage students to see themselves in a positive light and accept themselves for who they are, not who they feel they should be
- To show students how to transform the Act Like a Girl and Act Like a Boy Boxes and define their personal standards of dignity
- To allow students to reflect on and discuss their experiences in the program

MATERIALS

- Paper and pen/pencils
- Copies of the "I Am . . ." handout (see Appendix K)

Session Outline

What Are We Doing Today?

We are learning what we think was worthwhile in *Owning Up*.

Review It

Time: 5–10 minutes

What was one idea you thought about or someone said in last session's class that was most important in understanding sexual harassment and how people communicate in uncomfortable situations?

ACTIVITY: I Am . . .

Time: 10 minutes

Purpose: To focus on students' positive attributes and insights they have learned in the program

Say: We have spent a lot of time together, and now we are going to take the opportunity to answer some questions about how we see ourselves. To do this, I am going to give you some sentence stems and ask you to complete them in a positive way (see Appendix K for a handout).

> I am . . .
>
> I enjoy . . .
>
> I am happy when . . .
>
> I like the fact that I am . . .
>
> I am most proud about . . .
>
> My personal mantra/motto is. . . .

After the students have finished, give them an opportunity to share their responses in the overall group or break them into small groups, depending on their rapport.

ACTIVITY: Thinking About the *Owning Up* Experience

Time: 10–20 minutes

Purpose: To generate a discussion with students about their experiences in the program, using the following questions as a guide

Say: We've come a long way since the beginning of the *Owning Up* program. I have learned a lot, and I hope you have too. I have some questions to ask you to see what you thought about the program. So, we are going to play a game. Each of the questions is numbered. I am going to ask you the questions by rolling two dice. *(You can also do this with smaller groups and have them roll two dice.)* Whatever number you get is the question you answer.

1. What did you expect these sessions would be like? How were the sessions different from what you expected?
2. Are there any ways in which you see the world differently because of what we discussed in this program?
3. What were the most helpful topics we covered? How were these topics helpful to you?
4. What were the least helpful topics we covered? Why were these topics not as helpful to you?

5. Were there topics that we should have covered in a different way in the program? How should we have covered those topics?

6. What topics didn't we cover that we should include in the program?

7. What was the most difficult moment for you in the program?

8. What was the most meaningful moment for you in the program?

9. A year from now, what do you think you will best remember about the program?

Thank you for your feedback; it will make me a better instructor.

ACTIVITY: Carrying It Forward

Time: 15 minutes

Every person in this group can do something to solve a problem or advocate for a cause they think is important. And every person can use skills you learned in this program to help you achieve your goals. That could mean working with a group you're already involved in, finding a new issue you're passionate about, or finding a creative outlet for yourself. Some specific examples to get you thinking could be:

- School newspaper: work to represent differing opinions
- Student council: work to make all students feel welcome at dances or other school events
- Support diverse groups in your school
- Try out something new
- Support younger students

I am going to give you an index card and you're going to write down at least one answer about how you will make a difference. After we are all done, we are going to tape them to the board all together.

Debrief/Takeaways

Achieving these kinds of goals can be hard. If we support one another and use what we learned in this program, we have a much better chance of success.

Wrap It Up

Time: 10 minutes

- It's not hard to live according to your values when you like people. It's when you don't—yet still live according to your values—that it really matters.
- Your dignity is not negotiable. You have the right to have your voice heard, and so does everyone else.
- We expect great things from you.

Instructions: Below is a list of statements and numbers. Read the statement, then circle the number that matches what you think about that statement.

1 = Strongly Disagree

2 = Disagree

3 = Don't Know/Never Thought About It

4 = Agree

5 = Strongly Agree

EXAMPLE:

Playing video games is a fun thing to do.	1	2	3	4	⑤

You strongly agree that playing video games is a fun thing to do.

Survey:

1. I feel accepted by my community.	1	2	3	4	5
2. I feel comfortable standing up for something I believe in.	1	2	3	4	5
3. I feel comfortable intervening when I see someone being treated badly.	1	2	3	4	5
4. If I need help with a problem, I know an adult I can trust to help me.	1	2	3	4	5
5. I am able to have likes, dislikes, and social interactions independent of what my friends feel.	1	2	3	4	5
6. I believe apologizing is a sign of weakness.	1	2	3	4	5
7. If I hear a joke about someone's race, religion, or appearance, I have a strategy to address it.	1	2	3	4	5
8. I have a strategy to resolve conflicts I have with friends.	1	2	3	4	5
9. I can identify ways in which gender is defined by society.	1	2	3	4	5
10. I can identify situations in which I have been a bystander.	1	2	3	4	5
11. I know the difference between fun teasing and malicious teasing.	1	2	3	4	5
12. I can recognize examples of stereotyping that happen with my friends, in my school, or my community.	1	2	3	4	5
13. I understand the kinds of gossip that can be hurtful.	1	2	3	4	5
14. I have a personal understanding of the word *dignity*.	1	2	3	4	5
15. I hide aspects of my personality to please others.	1	2	3	4	5
16. I can identify ways that the media influence my style and behavior.	1	2	3	4	5
17. I believe my style reflects my authentic self.	1	2	3	4	5
18. I feel pressure to share the same style as my friends or others in my community.	1	2	3	4	5
19. I believe my social media profiles reflect my real and true self.	1	2	3	4	5

(Continued)

(Continued)

20. I feel pressure to maintain a certain image on my social media profiles.   1   2   3   4   5

21. I understand the impact social media can have on the way I see others.   1   2   3   4   5

22. I feel pressure to look a certain way because of my gender.   1   2   3   4   5

23. I believe boys can be sexually harassed.   1   2   3   4   5

24. No matter what race you are, racial stereotypes affect people's opinions and actions toward other people.   1   2   3   4   5

25. It is important to understand how race, gender, and ethnicity can impact the way people treat one another.   1   2   3   4   5

26. I can tell a friend when I think they are in a relationship that is not good for them.   1   2   3   4   5

27. It's mean to tell someone to be less physically affectionate with you.   1   2   3   4   5

28. I can tell my closest friends my true feelings.   1   2   3   4   5

WHO ARE YOU?

Grade:

Age:

Gender (male, female, other, prefer not to answer):

The following three questions are to be included only in the posttest:

Think about a time when you were angry with a friend. Describe that scenario, and explain how some of the strategies you learned in *Owning Up* would help you address a similar situation in the future.

In what ways are your social media choices an accurate representation of your life and your classmates' lives? In what ways are they not an accurate representation?

If you were in charge of changing any session of *Owning Up,* which session would it be? How would you change it?

Dear Parents or Guardians: Welcome to the new school year!

We are committed to creating a school culture where everyone is treated with dignity. To make this possible, we recognize that one of our most important responsibilities is to create and sustain a safe environment so our students can enjoy learning and focus on their work. As in any school, we acknowledge that social conflicts and bullying can occur within our community.

We also know that some of these issues can be complicated to define, and people have different thresholds for what bothers them. Even if it's not bullying, our students can get into conflicts with each other that can make it more difficult to learn. So while we work with teachers to create a safe learning environment in their classrooms, we also have the following programs and resources to support our students' social skills in their interactions with each other:

- Orientation program for younger students
- Peer advisors
- *Owning Up* (or a similar program)

If you have any questions about any of these programs, please don't hesitate to ask.

How do we define *bullying?* Bullying takes place when one person and/or a group of people repeatedly abuse or threaten to abuse their power over another person. This behavior has a profoundly negative impact both on an individual child's life and on the overall school culture. Bullying is a process of stripping someone of their dignity, of their inherent worth, by attacking and/or humiliating them because of a perceived inherent trait like their sexual orientation, their conformance to gender expectations, their religion, their socioeconomic level, their race, or a disability.

Where does bullying occur?

Bullying often occurs outside of the physical school grounds, yet these actions impact the safety of our students as though they occur on school grounds.

How will the school respond to bullying?

Any bullying behavior demonstrated at school or outside of school that affects our school community will be addressed by the school. As a school, we will take any report of bullying seriously. Bullying will be responded to through a continuum of consequences and interventions up to and including suspension and/or social probation, depending on the frequency and severity of the behavior.

Some situations, including less severe first offenses, may be handled by the school through student conferences, mediation, or other interventions without a phone call to the

(Continued)

(Continued)

student's parent(s) or guardian. If more serious bullying behavior has occurred, possible consequences could be suspension or expulsion from participation on a sports team or in other school activities. No matter how important your child is to the success of the team, play, or other school activity, his or her participation is a privilege, not a right. Subsequent consequences could include school suspension or expulsion. Any student who is suspended will not be permitted to return to school without a reentry meeting with an administrator. If any of these consequences becomes a likely outcome, we will notify you.

How can families respond to bullying and support the school?

If your child is the target of bullying inside or outside of school, please ask your child to describe the situation in writing. Please give us your contact information, including the best times to reach you. We will address any problems of this nature as quickly as possible, but please allow us 24 hours upon receipt of your written communication to respond. If you do not hear from us by that time, please feel free to call (specify appropriate person) to follow up.

Please understand that we want all our students to feel valued and respected in our school. These situations are hard for everyone—parents/guardians, school administrators, and students alike—but it is in these moments when we truly show what we stand for as a community. Working together, we can do our best to ensure that our school is a safe community where every child can succeed.

Thank you,
Your principal/administrator

Dear Mr. or Ms. Smith:

As you know, our school is committed to the well-being and safety of all our students. As a result, we take bullying behavior very seriously because it affects a student's experience at school and undermines our community as a whole. Unfortunately, it has come to my attention that your child has been involved in a bullying incident.

Description of events: Provide the facts of the situation, including concrete examples without judgments. Explain why the student's behavior is against the school's rules.

The request: Describe the next step in the process. For example:

Because of these actions, we request that your child write down his or her understanding of the events that led to this situation. We will follow this letter with a phone call or e-mail to schedule a meeting with you and (specify appropriate school personnel). This meeting will include (your child, a counselor, etc.).

The affirmation: We value your child as a student in our school and a member of our community, and we believe he or she can work with us to resolve this problem. We also want you to know that we would take similar measures to protect your child if he or she were the target of bullying.

With your help and cooperation, we have every expectation that this situation will be resolved in a mutually respectful manner. Please feel free to contact me with any concerns. I will get back to you as soon as possible.

Sincerely,
Your principal/administrator

Dear Principal Anderson:

My name is Mike Clark, and my son, Scott, is in Ms. Prescott's sixth-grade class.

Description of events:

Focus on:

- *When did the bullying incident occur?*
- *Where did it occur?*
- *Who was involved in the incident?*
- *Were there any witnesses?*
- *How has this incident affected your child?*
- *Have there been other similar incidents before this one?*
- *What steps have you taken to work on this issue?*

Example: I am writing today because my son came home last night telling me that he is being bullied by a group of kids in his class. Prior to this conversation, my wife and I noticed that Scott's attitude toward school had changed. He frequently complained of stomachaches and asked not to attend school. Finally, he admitted to us that two students in his class posted a humiliating picture they took of him during lunch. Scott doesn't want to go to school and can't concentrate enough to do his homework. We have already talked to Ms. Prescott, and she says she is trying to stop the behavior but that she can't control what the children do and say outside of the classroom.

The request:

Focus on:

- *What specific action(s) do you want the school to take?*
- *How would you like to be involved in the process?*

Example: I am requesting that you work with us so that Scott can feel safe at school and specifically in Ms. Prescott's class.

The affirmation:

Focus on:

- *What are you willing to do to help with the issue?*
- *How can the school best contact you?*

Example: I am eager to work with you and greatly appreciate the difficulty of these situations. I can be reached at (e-mail address here). Thank you for your consideration of this matter and working with us to create a solution.

Sincerely,
Mike Clark

What, for you, are the most important characteristics someone should have in order to be a good friend?

How would someone would treat you were you not to consider that friendship particularly strong or dependable?

Think about the quality of your friendships: Do they measure up to what you say you need? Are you treating people according to what you say you value in a friendship?

What were the popular clothes when you were my age?

What music did you like to listen to?

How did you decorate your room? For example, what posters did you have up on your walls?

Were there any students who stuck out at your school? How did people treat them?

Tell me about your friends when you were in school.

Did you have a really close friend? Why did you like this person?

What was your favorite thing to do with your friend(s)?

Did a friend ever do something behind your back—lie or gossip about you? What did they say?

How did you find out, and what did you do?

Did you ever spread rumors about, exclude, or ignore a friend? Why?

Were you confronted about doing this? What happened?

Were you ever teased or made fun of in school? How did you handle it?

Did you have a reputation in school? What was it? Did you like it?

Tell me about something you did when you were my age that you are most proud of now.

Act Like a Girl

Act Like a Boy

Available for download at **www.owningup.online**

152

APPENDIX H. Questions for the Beach Ball Exercise

What is the house or family chore you hate doing the most?

What is your favorite candy?

What would you rather do, scuba dive with sharks or skydive out of an airplane?

Who is your favorite superhero or superheroine?

Where were your parents born?

What is the food you hate the most?

What is a movie you want to see (or have seen) more than two times?

What is your favorite color of shoes?

What is your favorite dessert?

If you could go anywhere in the world, where would it be?

If you had a superpower, what would it be?

What's your favorite school lunch food?

What's your least favorite school lunch food?

If there was a place in the school that was haunted, where would it be?

Queen Bee/Mastermind

Charismatic/fun

Looks confident

Has the final say about what the group does and likes

Others want their approval

Intimidating

Sidekick/Associate

Gatekeeper to the Queen Bee or Mastermind

Can be jealous of others' relationships with the Queen Bee or Mastermind

Has strong opinions about who should or shouldn't be in the group

Banker

Good at getting information from people

Spreads gossip, but doesn't get caught

Reads people easily

Messenger

Wants people to get along

Doesn't like conflict

Brings information to people in the group who are angry at each other

Conscience

Rule follower

Worries about getting in trouble

Adults like them

To the other people in the group, it can feel like they're a chaperone or a parent

The Bouncer

Doesn't read other people well

Does other people's dirty work

Believes showing loyalty to other people in the group is very important

Pleaser/Fly

Hovers outside the group

Tries to get people to like them by showing off

People in the group usually don't feel bad about being mean to them because it looks like they're asking for it

Peacemaker/Entertainer

Distracts people when there's a conflict in the group

Makes jokes to smooth conflicts over in the group

Gets along with people in other groups

Punching Bag

People in the group genuinely like them, but they're an easy target for relentless teasing by others in the group

Friends don't take what they do to them seriously—even if they know they hate it

Apologize/make excuses to others outside the group about how they're treated

The Keystone

Doesn't believe that their identity is tied to the group

Challenges the person who is being mean

Doesn't change their opinion to please other people

APPENDIX J. Eating Disorders Handout

Types of Eating Disorders

- Anorexia
- Bulimia
- Binge Eating Disorder
- Other Specified Feeding or Eating Disorder (OSFED)

Eating Disorders Myths and Facts

Myth: It's obvious when someone has an eating disorder.

Fact: Eating disorders are not always obvious. The media often portray individuals with an eating disorder as extremely underweight and malnourished, which isn't always accurate. Individuals suffering from anorexia can be normal or overweight, and individuals suffering from binge eating disorder can be underweight.

Myth: Eating disorders are just about food.

Fact: Eating disorders are serious mental disorders. Control or lack of control over food is a manifestation of the disorder.

Myth: People with anorexia don't eat.

Fact: Again, food is a symptom of an eating disorder. Many people with anorexia have eating rituals or behaviors as an attempt to gain control over a particular area of their life. Just because someone is eating doesn't mean they are not suffering.

Myth: Eating disorders afflict only girls and women.

Fact: Eating disorders don't discriminate against gender, age, race, ethnicity, socioeconomic status, or anything else. Anyone can suffer from an eating disorder.

Myth: Eating disorders are a choice.

Fact: Eating disorders are biologically based illnesses and not a choice.

Myth: Recovery from an eating disorder is simple.

Fact: Recovering from an eating disorder is complex and often involves a treatment team of a counselor, physician, and dietician.

Red Flags

- Preoccupation with food, weight, and/or appearance
- Frequent concerns about weight
- Spending too much time exercising
- Social disengagement
- Skipping meals
- Lying about food intake
- Food rituals (cutting food into small pieces, excessive chewing, etc.)
- Missing food
- Hoarding food

(Continued)

155

(Continued)

- Becoming overly upset when food is missing
- Preoccupation with what other people are eating
- Disordered view of self
- Denial of hunger

What to Do if You Suspect a Friend Has an Eating Disorder

- Gather information about eating disorders from qualified resources.
- Confront your friend in a confidential setting; express concern in a loving and supportive way.
- Point out behaviors to avoid blame or shame. For example, "I notice you're spending a lot of time running and haven't been hanging out much. What's going on?" or "You've been avoiding us at lunch and I'm worried. What's going on?"
- If your friend admits to having an eating disorder, encourage them to get help and talk to a trusted adult (parent, school counselor, coach, teacher, etc.).
- Avoid making comments about your body shape/size, food, dieting, or weight loss or gain.
- Try to avoid making situations awkward. Keep inviting your friend to social functions, even if they refuse to go. Set boundaries and remember that you are not responsible for your friend's eating disorder. You cannot fix it, but you can always be there for support.
- Talk to someone if you need to. Eating disorders are tricky, and you might find yourself needing support as well.

What to Do if You Have an Eating Disorder

- Tell somebody—a parent, trusted adult, school counselor, teacher, friend, or professional. You cannot heal from an eating disorder alone. Ask to talk when you both have some time and are not in a hurry.
- Practice what you are going to say. Write it down, say it aloud, or go over it in your head.
- Many adults do not understand eating disorders. Don't be discouraged if people are shocked, deny the problem, or get angry. Be proud of yourself for coming forward, and remember that you deserve to be healthy and happy.
- Remember that eating disorders are not about food, size, weight, or shape. Food/weight preoccupations and obsessions are merely symptoms. Ask for help from a qualified professional who has experience with eating disorders/body image concerns.
- Be honest about your needs. Eating disorders are difficult to treat, and you will need a lot of support. Ask for help and be specific about your needs.

Source: Adapted from National Eating Disorders Association (http://www.nationaleatingdisorders.org).

I am . . .

I enjoy . . .

I am happy when . . .

I like the fact that I am . . .

I am most proud about . . .

My personal mantra/motto is. . . .

Resources

Support for Educators

Are We Closing the School Discipline Gap? by Daniel Losen, Cheri Hodson, Michael A. Keith II, Katrina Morrison, and Shakit Belway. The Center for Civil Rights Remedies, 2015.

Behind the Counselor's Door: Teenagers' True Confessions, Trials, and Triumphs, by Kevin Kuczynski. Health Communications, 2015.

Breaking Through to Teens: A New Psychotherapy for New Adolescence, by Ron Taffel. Guilford Press, 2005.

Getting Through to Difficult Kids and Parents: Uncommon Sense for Child Professionals, by Ron Taffel. Guilford Press, 2004.

Girls in Real-Life Situations: Group Counseling for Enhancing Social and Emotional Development (Grades K–5), by Shannon Trice-Black and Julia V. Taylor. Research Press, 2007. (Curriculum)

Girls in Real-Life Situations: Group Counseling for Enhancing Social and Emotional Development (Grades 6–12), by Julia V. Taylor and Shannon Trice-Black. Research Press, 2007. (Curriculum)

An Improbable School: Transforming How Teachers Teach and Students Learn, by Paul Tweed and Liz Seubert. Lead the Path, 2015.

The Motivation Breakthrough: 6 Secrets to Turning on the Tuned-Out Child, by Richard Lavoie. Touchstone, 2008.

What Works for Teens: A Professional's Guide to Engaging Authentically With Adolescents to Achieve Lasting Change, by Britt H. Rathbone and Julie Baron. New Harbinger, 2015.

Working With Parents: Building Relationships for Student Success, by Ruby K. Payne. aha! Process, Inc., 2005.

Working With Students: Discipline Strategies for the Classroom, by Ruby K. Payne. aha! Process, Inc., 2006.

Support for Parents

The Blessing of a Skinned Knee: Using Jewish Teachings to Raise Self-Reliant Children, by Wendy Mogel. Scribner, 2008.

Childhood Unbound: Saving Our Kids' Best Selves—Confident Parenting in a World of Change, by Ron Taffel. Free Press, 2009.

The Good Enough Teen: Raising Adolescents With Love and Acceptance, Despite How Impossible They Can Be, by Brad E. Sachs. Harper Paperbacks, 2005.

The Pecking Order: Which Siblings Succeed and Why, by Dalton Conley. Pantheon, 2004.

The Pressured Child: Helping Your Child Find Success in School and Life, by Michael G. Thompson and Teresa Barker. Ballantine Books, 2005.

Queen Bee Moms and Kingpin Dads: Dealing With the Difficult Parents in Your Child's Life, by Rosalind Wiseman and Elizabeth Rapoport. Three Rivers Press, 2007.

Teach Your Children Well: Why Values and Coping Skills Matter More Than Grades, Trophies, or "Fat Envelopes," by Madeline Levine. Harper Perennial, 2013.

When Parents Disagree and What You Can Do About It, by Ron Taffel. Guilford Press, 2002.

Worried All the Time: Overparenting in an Age of Anxiety and How to Stop It, by David Anderegg. Free Press, 2003.

Cultural Commentary and Critique

Can't Stop Won't Stop: A History of the Hip-Hop Generation, by Jeff Chang. St. Martin's Press, 2005.

Freaks, Geeks, and Cool Kids: American Teenagers, Schools, and the Culture of Consumption, by Murray Milner Jr. Routledge, 2004.

Goth: Undead Subculture, by Lauren M. E. Goodlad and Michael Bibby, eds. Duke University Press, 2007.

The Nature of Prejudice: 25th Anniversary, by Gordon W. Allport. Perseus Book Group, 1979.

Nerds: Who They Are and Why We Need More of Them, by David Anderegg. Tarcher, 2007.

Teens Take It to Court: Young People Who Challenged the Law and Changed Your Life, by Judge Tom Jacobs. Free Spirit, 2006.

Bullying, Social Justice, and Intervention Strategies

All Rise: Somebodies, Nobodies, and the Politics of Dignity, by Robert Fuller. Berrett-Koehler, 2006.

Best Friends, Worst Enemies: Understanding the Social Lives of Children, by Michael Thompson, Catherine O'Neill Grace, and Lawrence J. Cohen. Ballantine Books, 2002.

Bullying From Both Sides: Strategic Interventions for Working With Bullies and Victims, by Walter B. Roberts Jr. Corwin, 2005.

Letters to a Bullied Girl: Messages of Healing and Hope, by Olivia Gardner, Emily Buder, and Sarah Buder. Harper Paperbacks, 2008.

Mom, They're Teasing Me: Helping Your Child Solve Social Problems, by Michael G. Thompson, Lawrence J. Cohen, and Catherine O'Neill. Ballantine Books, 2004.

Please Stop Laughing at Me: One Woman's Inspirational Story, by Jodee Blanco. Adams Media, 2003.

Safe School Ambassadors: Harnessing Student Power to Stop Bullying and Violence, by Rick Phillips, John Linney, and Chris Pack. Jossey-Bass, 2008. (Curriculum)

Salvaging Sisterhood, by Julia V. Taylor. Youthlight, 2005. (Curriculum)

Sticks and Stones: Defeating the Culture of Bullying and Rediscovering the Power of Character and Empathy, by Emily Bazelon. Random House, 2013.

Youth Voice Project: Student Insights Into Bullying and Peer Mistreatment, by Stan David and Charisse Nixon. Research Press, 2014.

Brain Development and Puberty

Age of Opportunity: Lessons From the New Science of Adolescence, by Laurence Steinberg. Houghton Mifflin Harcourt, 2014.

Brainstorm: The Power and Purpose of the Teenage Brain, by Daniel Siegal. Tarcher, 2015.

The New Puberty: How to Navigate Early Development in Today's Girls, by Louise Greenspan and Julianna Deardoff. Rodale, 2015.

NurtureShock: New Thinking About Children, by Po Bronson and Ashley Merryman. Twelve, 2011.

The Teenage Brain: A Neuroscientist's Survival Guide to Raising Adolescents and Young Adults, by Frances Jensen. Harper, 2015.

What's Happening to Ellie?: A Book About Puberty for Girls and Young Women With Autism and Related Conditions, by Kate E. Reynolds. Jessica Kingsley Publishers, 2015.

The Whole-Brain Child: 12 Revolutionary Strategies to Nurture Your Child's Developing Mind, by Daniel Siegal and Tina Payne Bryson. Delacorte Press, 2011.

Learning Differences

Delivered From Distraction: Getting the Most Out of Life With Attention Deficit Disorder, by Edward M. Hallowell and John J. Ratey. Ballantine Books, 2005.

Driven to Distraction: Recognizing and Coping With Attention Deficit Disorder From Childhood Through Adulthood, by Edward M. Hallowell and John J. Ratey. Touchstone, 1995.

The Girls' Guide to ADHD, by Beth Walker. Woodbine House, 2004.

It's So Much Work to Be Your Friend: Helping the Child With Learning Disabilities Find Social Success, by Richard Lavoie. Touchstone, 2006.

Key Indicators of Child Well-Being: Completing the Picture, by Brett Brown, ed. Lawrence Erlbaum, 2007.

The Motivation Breakthrough, by Richard Lavoie. Gerardine Wurzburg (Director). PBS Video, 2007.

Thinking in Pictures and Other Reports From My Life With Autism, by Temple Grandin. Vintage Books, 1996.

Understanding Girls With ADHD: Updated and Revised—How They Feel and Why They Do What They Do, by Kathleen Nadeau and Ellen Littman. Advantage, 2015.

Reflections on Acting Like a Girl

The Blueprint for My Girls: How to Build a Life Full of Courage, Determination and Self-Love, by Yasmin Shiraz. Fireside, 2004.

The Born Frees, Writing With the Girls of Gugulethu, by Kimberly Burge. Norton, 2015.

Cinderella Ate My Daughter: Dispatches From the Front Lines of Girly-Girl Culture, by Peggy Orenstein. Harper, 2012.

The Curse of the Good Girl: Raising Authentic Girls With Courage and Confidence, by Rachel Simmons. Penguin Press, 2009.

Express Yourself: A Teen Girl's Guide to Speaking Up and Being Who You Are, by Emily Roberts. Instant Help Books, 2015.

Female Chauvinist Pigs: Women and the Rise of Raunch Culture, by Ariel Levy. Free Press, 2005.

Full of Ourselves: A Wellness Program to Advance Girl Power, Health, and Learning, by Catherine Seiner-Adair and Lisa Sjostrom. Teachers College Press, 2006. (Curriculum)

Girls and Sex: Navigating the Complicated New Landscape, by Peggy Orenstein. Harper, 2016.

Girls on Track: A Parent's Guide to Inspiring Our Daughters to Achieve a Lifetime of Self-Esteem and Respect, by Molly Barker. Random House, 2004.

Manifesta: Young Women, Feminism, and the Future, by Jennifer Baumgardner and Amy Richards. Farrar, Straus and Giroux, 2000.

Meeting at the Crossroads: Women's Psychology and Girls' Development, by Lyn Mikel Brown and Carol Gilligan. Harvard University Press, 1998.

Odd Girl Out: The Hidden Culture of Girls' Aggression, by Rachel Simmons. Harcourt, 2002.

Odd Girl Speaks Out: Girls Write About Bullies, Cliques, Popularity, and Jealousy, by Rachel Simmons. Harcourt, 2004.

Ophelia Speaks: Adolescent Girls Write About Their Search for Self, by Sara Shandler. Harper Perennial, 2000.

Ophelia's Mom: Women Speak Out About Loving and Letting Go of Their Adolescent Daughters, by Nina Shandler. Crown, 2001.

Packaging Girlhood: Rescuing Our Daughters From Marketing Schemes, by Sharon Lamb and Lyn Mikel Brown. St. Martin's Press, 2006.

Redefining Girly: How Parents Can Fight the Stereotyping and Sexualizing of Girlhood From Birth to Tween, by Melissa Atkins Wardy. Chicago Review Press, 2014.

Reviving Ophelia: Saving the Selves of Adolescent Girls, by Mary Pipher. Ballantine Books, 1994.

School Girls: Young Women, Self-Esteem, and the Confidence Gap, by Peggy Orenstein. Doubleday, 1994.

See Jane Hit: Why Girls Are Growing More Violent and What Can Be Done About It, by James Garbarino. Penguin Press, 2006.

See Jane Win: The Rimm Report on How 1,000 Girls Became Successful Women, by Silvia Rimm. Three Rivers Press, 1999.

A Smart Girl's Guide: Drama, Rumors, and Secrets, by Nancy Holyoke. American Girl, 2015.

Stressed-Out Girls: Helping Them Thrive in an Age of Pressure, by Roni Cohen-Sandler. Penguin Press, 2005.

Untangled: Guiding Teenage Girls Through the Seven Transitions Into Adulthood, by Lisa Damour. Ballantine, 2016.

You Can't Say You Can't Play, by Vivian Gussin Paley. Harvard University Press, 1993.

Media and Technology

Adolescents, Media, and the Law: What Developmental Science Reveals and Free Speech Requires, by Roger J. R. Levesque. Oxford University Press, 2007.

The Big Disconnect: Protecting Childhood and Family Relationships in the Digital Age, by Catherine Steiner Adair and Teresa Barker. Harper, 2014.

Consuming Kids: The Commercialization of Childhood, by Adriana Barbaro and Jeremy Ear (Directors). Media Education Foundation, 2008. (www.mediaed.org)

The Games Believe in You: How Games Can Make Our Kids Smarter, by Greg Toppo. Palgrave, 2015.

It's Complicated: The Social Lives of Networked Teens, by danah boyd. Yale University Press, 2015.

Killing Us Softly: Advertising's Image of Women, by Jean Kilbourne. Sut Jhally (Director). Media Education Foundation, 2006. (www.mediaed.org)

Reality Is Broken: Why Games Make Us Better and How They Can Change the World, by Jane McGonigal. Penguin, 2011.

The Second Family: Dealing With Peer Power, Pop Culture, the Wall of Silence, and Other Challenges of Raising Today's Teen, by Ron Taffel. St. Martin's Griffin, 2002.

"Sexting as Media Production: Rethinking Social Media and Sexuality," by A. A. Hasinoff. *New Media & Society 15,* no. 4 (2012): 449–465. doi:10.1177/1461444812459171

Race, Ethnicity, and Diversity

All About Love: New Visions, by bell hooks. William Morrow, 2000.

Bridges Out of Poverty, by Philip DeVol, Terie Dreussi Smith, and Ruby K. Payne. aha! Process, Inc., 2006.

The Color of Success: Race and High-Achieving Urban Youth, by Gilberto Q. Conchas. Teachers College Press, 2006.

A Framework for Understanding Poverty, by Ruby K. Payne. aha! Process, Inc., 2005.

Hidden Rules of Class at Work, by Ruby K. Payne and Don L. Krabill. aha! Process, Inc., 2002.

Hip-Hop: Beyond Beats and Rhymes (abridged), by Byron Hurt (Director). Media Education Foundation, 2006. (www.mediaed.org)

Hopeful Girls, Troubled Boys: Race and Gender Disparity in Urban Education, by Nancy Lopez. Routledge, 2002.

Possibilities for Moving Theory to Practice in Urban Schools, by Jeffrey M. R. Duncan-Andrade and Ernest Morrell. Peter Lang, 2008.

Race in the Schoolyard: Negotiating the Color Line in Classrooms and Communities, by Amanda E. Lewis. Rutgers University Press, 2003.

School Kids/Street Kids: Identity Development in Latino Students, by Nilda Flores-Gonzalez. Teachers College Press, 2002.

Under-Resourced Learners: 8 Strategies to Boost Student Achievement, by Ruby K. Payne and Dan Shenk. aha! Process, Inc., 2008.

Up Against Whiteness: Race, School and Immigrant Youth, by Stacey J. Lee. Teachers College Press, 2005.

Urban Girls Revisited: Building Strengths, by Bonnie Leadbeater and Niobe Way. New York University Press, 2007.

We Can't Teach What We Don't Know: White Teachers, Multiracial Schools, by Gary R. Howard. Teachers College Press, 2006.

"Why Are All the Black Kids Sitting Together in the Cafeteria?" And Other Conversations About Race, by Beverly Daniel Tatum. Basic Books, 2003.

Why White Kids Love Hip-Hop: Wangstas, Wiggers, Wannabes, and the New Reality of Race in America, by Bakari Kitwana. Basic Civitas Books, 2005.

Women Without Class: Girls, Race, and Identity, by Julie Bettie. University of California Press, 2002.

Body Image and Eating Disorders

The Body Image Workbook for Teens: Activities to Help Girls Develop a Healthy Body in an Image-Obsessed World, by Julia Taylor. Instant Help, 2014.

The Cult of Thinness, by Sharlene Nagy Hesse-Biber. Oxford University Press, 2007.

The Geography of Girlhood, by Kirsten Smith. Little, Brown Young Readers, 2007.

Go Figure, by Jo Edwards. Simon Pulse, 2007.

Locker Room Diaries: The Naked Truth About Women, Body Image, and Re-imagining the "Perfect" Body, by Leslie Goldman. Da Capo Press, 2007.

Packaging Girlhood: Rescuing Our Daughters From Marketers' Schemes, by Sharon Lamb and Lyn Mikel Brown. St. Martin's Griffin, 2007.

Sexuality

Adolescent Sexuality: A Historical Handbook and Guide, by Carolyn Cocca, ed. Praeger, 2006.

Becoming Nicole: The Transformation of an American Family, by Amy Ellis Nutt. Random House, 2015.

Everything You Never Wanted Your Kids to Know About Sex (But Were Afraid They'd Ask): The Secret to Surviving Your Child's Sexual Development From Birth to the Teens, by Justin Richardson and Mark A. Schuster. Crown, 2003.

From Teasing to Torment: School Climate in America—A Survey of Students and Teachers, by Dana Markow and Jordan Fein (Harris Interactive). Gay, Lesbian and Straight Education Network, 2005 (http://www.glsenboston.org/GLSENFromTeasingToTorment.pdf)

National School Climate Survey: The Experiences of Lesbian, Gay, Bisexual and Transgender Youth in Our Nation's Schools, by Joseph G. Kosciw and Elizabeth M. Diaz. Gay, 2015.

"Seeing and Being Seen: Co-situation and Impression Formation Using Grindr, a Location-Aware Gay Dating App," by C. Blackwell, J. Birnholtz, and C. Abbott. *New Media & Society 17,* no. 7 (2014): 1117–1136. doi:10.1177/1461444814521595

Some Assembly Required: The Not-So-Secret Life of a Transgender Teen, by Arin Andrews. Simon & Schuster, 2014.

Sexual Assault and Abusive Relationships

But He'll Change: End the Thinking That Keeps You in an Abusive Relationship, by Joanna V. Hunter. Hazeldon, 2010.

Giving Yourself Permission: A Guide to Reclaiming Your Life After Sexual Assault, by Shaneequa Cannon. Amazon Digital Services, 2015.

I Will Survive: The African-American Guide to Healing From Sexual Assault and Abuse, by Lori Robinson. Seal Press, 2003.

Sexual Assault: Techniques and Exercises to Help You Heal, by Violet Daniels and Joanna Scribe. Amazon Digital Services, 2013.

The Sexual Trauma Workbook for Teen Girls: A Guide to Recovery From Sexual Assault and Abuse, by Raychelle Cassada Lohman and Sheela Raja. Instant Help, 2016.

Should I Stay or Should I Go?: A Guide to Knowing if Your Relationship Can—and Should—Be Saved, by Lundy Bancroft. Berkley, 2011.

Surviving the Silence: Black Women's Stories of Rape, by Charlotte Pierce-Baker. Norton, 2000.

Social and Emotional Learning

"The Economic Value of Social and Emotional Learning," by Clive Belfield, A. Brooks Bowden, Alli Klapp, Henry Levin, Robert Shand, and Sabine Zander. *Journal of Benefit-Cost Analysis 6,* no. 3 (2015): 508–544. doi:10.1017/bca.2015.55

"The Impact of Teasing and Bullying on Schoolwide Academic Performance," by Anna Lacey and Dewey Cornell. *Journal of Applied School Psychology 29,* no. 3 (2013): 262–283. doi:10.1080/1 5377903.2013.806883

Books for Younger Children

A Bad Case of Tattle Tongue, by Julia Cook. National Center for Youth Issues, 2006.

Bootsie Barker Bites, by Barbara Bottner. Putnam Juvenile, 1997.

Chrysanthemum, by Kevin Henkes. Greenwillow, 1991.

How to Lose All Your Friends, by Nancy Carlson. Puffin, 1997.

Just Kidding, by Trudy Ludwig. Tricycle Press, 2006.

Loud Emily, by Alexis O'Neill. Aladdin, 2001.

My Mouth Is a Volcano!, by Julia Cook. National Center for Youth Issues, 2008.

My Secret Bully, by Trudy Ludwig. Tricycle Press, 1995.

Odd Velvet, by Mary E. Whitcomb. Chronicle Books, 1998.

Pig Is Moving In, by Claudia Fries. Scholastic, 2000.

The Recess Queen, by Alexis O'Neill. Scholastic, 2005.

The Sneetches and Other Stories, by Dr. Seuss. Random House, 1961.

Sorry!, by Trudy Ludwig. Tricycle Press, 2006.

Stand Tall, Molly Lou Mellon, by Patty Lovell. Putnam Juvenile, 2006.

Too Perfect, by Trudy Ludwig and Lisa Fields. Tricycle Press, 2009.

Trouble Talk, by Trudy Ludwig and Mikela Prevost. Tricycle Press, 2008.

Worst Best Friend, by Alexis O'Neill. Scholastic Press, 2008.

Websites

About Face: www.about-face.org

American Civil Liberties Union LGBT Project: www.aclu.org/issues/lgbt-rights

Amy Poehler's Smart Girls: http://amysmartgirls.com

Anti-Defamation League: http://www.adl.org

Body Positive: www.bodypositive.com

Deadspin—Sports News Without Access, Favor, or Discretion: http://deadspin.com

Eating Disorder Referral and Network Center: www.edreferral.com

Education Week: http://www.edweek.org

Facing History and Ourselves: https://www.facinghistory.org

Gay and Lesbian Alliance Against Defamation: http://www.glaad.org

Gay Lesbian Straight Education Network: http://www.glsen.org

Girls' Online Magazine and Community: http://newmoon.com

Men Can Stop Rape: www.mencanstoprape.org

National Coalition Against Domestic Violence: www.ncadv.org

National Eating Disorders Association: www.nationaleatingdisorders.org

National Sexual Violence Resource Center: www.nsvrc.org

The Safe Schools Coalition: www.safeschoolscoalition.org

Teaching Tolerance—A Project of the Southern Poverty Law Center: www.tolerance.org

The World's Largest Collection of Books, Toys and Movies for Smart, Confident, Courageous Girls: http://amightygirl.org

YouTube Channels

SoulPancake

StyleLikeU

vlogbrothers

Notes

Notes

Notes

Notes

A SAGE Publishing Company

Helping educators make the greatest impact

CORWIN HAS ONE MISSION: to enhance education through intentional professional learning.

We build long-term relationships with our authors, educators, clients, and associations who partner with us to develop and continuously improve the best evidence-based practices that establish and support lifelong learning.

The Association for Middle Level Education is dedicated to improving the educational experiences of all students ages 10 to 15 by providing vision, knowledge, and resources to educators and leaders.

Solutions you want. Experts you trust. Results you need.

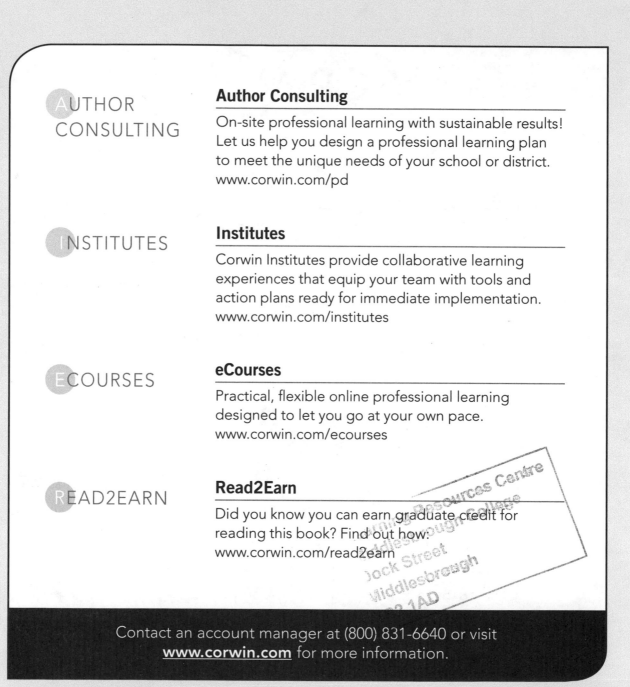